Advance praise

"Her travels through Kenya are enriched by an artist's eye, enabling her to capture the essence of the African bush. She sketches romantically both the colors and the texture of her natural surroundings. Heather's delicious description of her own sensory overload at the grandeur and her impressions of the changing bush, animals and birds, are authentic. "
~ *Chris Mercer, Dir. Campaign Against Canned Hunting* ~

"For many, a journey in East Africa will be confined to a safari park, while never allowing the opportunity to connect with the local culture. *Caught on the Equator* sheds valuable insight, far from the beaten path."
~ *Tim Gregory, Ex. Dir. ~ Kenya Connect (Charity for children)*

"Heather, I have been fascinated by your story from the first time you told me about your adventures...and what a great story for everyone, including our WomanTalk Live audience!"
~ *Ann Quasman -WomanTalk Live ~ 680 WCBM, Baltimore*

"To put it mildly- I 'm totally surprised and elated about your wonderful project! Kenya, the safari adventures, and the nearly endless rich experiences your book highlights will certainly bring joy and many laughs to your readers...!"
~ *Dr. Howard Erickson; Professor of Zoology- retired~ Towson University, Trip leader-1983*

"Heather is such a great writer, she truly captured the magic, splendor and paradox that was Africa. Tragically it is so quickly fading away. It was amazing to be transported back again....and I am sharing this book with my grandchildren!
~ Russ Harris ~ grandfather

Deb—

It has been
great knowing you—

All the Best,

Heather
Shum

June 13, 2013

CAUGHT ON THE EQUATOR

FINDING THE FIRE WITHIN

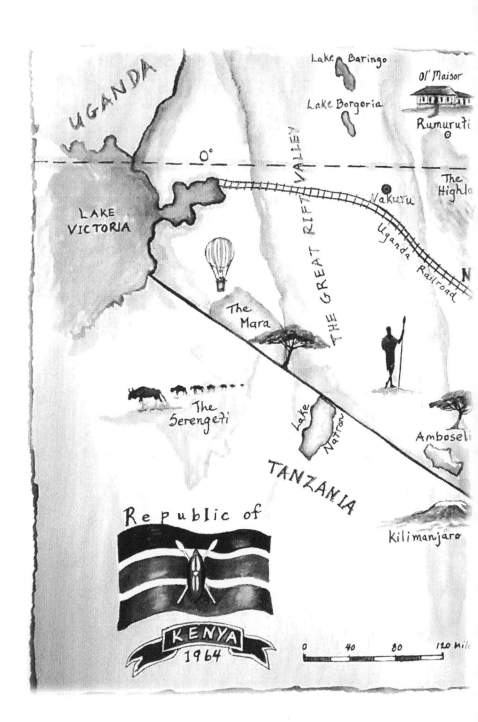

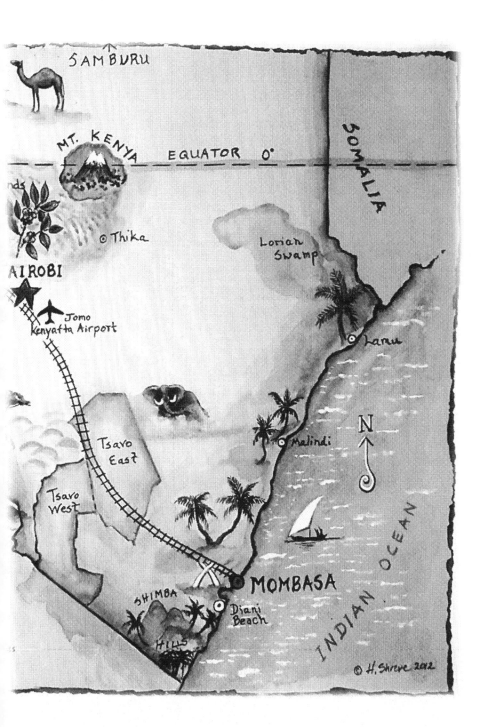

SAMBURU

MT. KENYA

EQUATOR 0°

SOMALIA

nds

Thika

Lorian Swamp

AIROBI

Jomo Kenyatta Airport

Lamu

N

Tsavo East

Malindi

Tsavo West

INDIAN OCEAN

MOMBASA

SHIMBA

Diani Beach

HILLS

© H. Shreve 2012

This book is dedicated to
my two children,
Emilia and Lee,
who remind me
every day
that beauty
and love
are endless.

CAUGHT ON THE EQUATOR

FINDING THE FIRE WITHIN

Written and Illustrated by
By Heather P. Shreve

"We cannot see

ourselves

clearly

until we

become

the fire."

~ H.P. Shreve ~

TABLE OF CONTENTS

FOREWORD
By Margrit Harris

"When we try to pick out anything by itself, we find it hitched to everything else in the universe."
~ John Muir ~

"They're all gone!" This stunning announcement by the Mozambique government came in late April 2013. The country's rhino population in Limpopo National Park has been decimated, shocking wildlife lovers everywhere. Daily reports continue to come out about African elephant herds being ravaged by military style hi-tech poachers, killing between 20,000 and 30,000 elephant each year for the bounty on their heads, their horn and tusks.

Born and raised in Africa, I experienced a unique era during my youth. For both Heather and I, years went by until we revisited our passion around Africa. Now, the time is here to turn our eyes back to this magnificent continent.

Heather's story goes far beyond being a good read for me. Her personal account takes us on a unique journey of the raw, wild beauty of Africa, punctuated by the continent's ever present mortal enemy; the poacher. Since 2010, I've been immersed in helping those who are actively working on the ground in South Africa to stop the poachers and via the social networks to end the demand for wildlife products.

Heather's remarkable experience in Africa in the 1980's takes us to a time, not so long ago, when Africa was teeming with wild animals and birds. An Africa that most of us are still fantasizing about, and one that is fading rapidly due to serious habitat loss and poaching. In the early 1980's, poaching was on the rise. Now, it's estimated that more than half of Africa's elephants were wiped out by the end of that decade. In 1990, an international ivory trade ban, plus a global awareness campaign, reversed the trend.

Unfortunately, around 2010, with new found wealth from younger generations (especially in Asia) there is hankering again for ivory, horn, lion bones and other wildlife body parts. With this demand, the poaching of elephant, rhino, lion and other wildlife has returned with a vengeance. Poaching, commonly referred to as wildlife trafficking, is a $19 billion dollar industry, ranking right up there with the illegal trade of drugs and guns.

The timing of *Caught on the Equator* may be serendipitous, as it allows us to journey with Heather into a beautiful world, which now stands on the brink of collapse. Her innocent story and inadvertent venture into the black market makes a spell-binding read, as well as being pertinently educational and informative.

By reading this book, you can help end the demand by being more aware of the products you buy. According to an address in late 2012 by US Secretary of State, Hillary Clinton, the USA is the second largest importer of illegally traded wildlife and wildlife products. From exotic pets to feathers, shoes, purses, jewelry and rugs that tantalize your fancy, these items may well have been poached from a forest in Central America or the African bush.

Although we might think it is hopeless to save Africa's wildlife from extinction, there is much that is being done by passionate and dedicated individuals and organizations. If Heather's story brings this topic to the forefront for one person, Heather will have accomplished her goal. If our beautiful Africa and its splendid wildlife are to survive, we need to join hands and collectively work to stop the poachers and end the demand.

Margrit Harris ~Wildlife Margrit
Founder and Executive Director of NIKELA
Helping People - Saving Wildlife
www.Nikela.org

INTRODUCTION

*"If you want to know who you are, don't ask— Act!
Let your actions delineate and define you."*
~ Thomas Jefferson ~

I was only nineteen and unsure; uncertain whether I would remember my sublime journey to East Africa in all her glory and detail. I took no notes, did no sketches and was without paper or brushes to record any part of my adventure. Except for a camera and my memory, I had left it all to chance.

If the images I had seen in Africa were with my eyes alone, I may not have remembered them so clearly. But my encounter with the equator was through my soul, and so all the beauty and the special music which came from her were captured in my heart, forever. Thirty years needed to pass before I truly understood her messages and could embrace the quiet whispers of Truth. It was a requirement of sorts for me to be able to describe adequately a place where north and south, light and dark, fire and ice collide in such spectacular form.

   None of us can see down the road of life enough to know that we have been protected from seeing too much. Only when we are ready, do we see the journey for what it was…and what it wasn't. In 1983, the portrait of my life was about to be tested. I see now that like a piece of canvas pulled round wooden strips, the strength always comes from the stretch.

   I often wonder if time will change the memories I left behind in Kenya. *Will the smiling lemon moon still shine as brightly on the azure sea? Will the joy of the river's flow still recount the secrets of life as it did for me? Will I still remember the song of Africa and hear her distant hum? Will I feel her perpetual fire for the rest of my days?*

   Decades have passed and the answers have been revealed slowly. One thing is for certain, my way into Africa was relatively simple. The way out was not.

Heattie P. Shrue

CHAPTER ONE

Drawn In ~ Over the Horizon

"The soul never thinks without a picture."

~ Plato ~

Nothing could have prepared me for this. As I pulled back the canvas tent flap, the smells that escaped swept over me like a wave. The aromas were earthy; sour goat's milk, acrid soils, smoke, and cattle dung. The words being spoken were extraordinary and primitive, like nothing I had ever experienced. The mixture of Maa and Swahili felt primal, like a snapshot of another time in human history. These exotic sounds and smells would live deep in my mind, lingering there as uniquely African, ready to be reawakened.

What lay before me was a testament to the talent of the Maasai. They took materials from the land and molded them into something special; excellent carvings, baskets, and jewelry. Even though I had just seen native crafts like this in Nairobi, these felt real, more authentic. Today, in this tent, on our way into the bush, my world would overlap the world of the Maasai, just for a moment.

"*Jambo*, Miss," they said, smiling and looking me in the face. "Can we help djou find someting?"

"Oh, no. I am OK, just looking."

As I wandered about, admiring the wide variety of traditional wood carvings, masks, drums, and wearable art, I was drawn to the animal carvings made from black *mpingo*, what we call ebony. It is still one of the most valuable woods in Africa and is sought after for its smooth texture. The Maasai are also are well-known for carving the native soap stone into spoons, figurines, chess sets, and more. I picked up a piece of the polished stone. The beautiful colors mimicked the hues of the dusty African soil — terra cottas, grays, creams, browns, and reds. So natural, I knew I would have to bring something home made from the *udongo wa Afrika.*

Then I saw the jewelry. The Maasai fashioned it from objects found in the bush: teeth, bone, braided cording, and wood. There were their traditional beaded yokes as well. Laid out on one of the tables were some solid white rings and one bracelet. Opaque, smooth, and creamy, they caught my eye. I picked them up one by one, inspected them, and put them back down. I

really liked the bracelet. Suddenly I felt someone
behind me. A Maasai herdsman who must have sensed
their appeal to me had approached me as I was about to
turn and go. He mumbled something in Swahili as he
quickly put the bracelet in the front pocket of my gray-
green safari jacket. I pulled it out of my pocket.

"Djou want dat bracelet, Miss? It's for djou." He
seemed anxious.

"Oh, OK," I said, slightly surprised. "Well, can I
trade you my jeans for it?"

"Oh, djes, Miss. Djes, *asante sana.*"

"Thank you." I said. "I'll take those rings, too."

"Dey are bone, djou know," he added with a big
smile.

I nodded, and gave him my broken watch that I
had also brought to trade. Bartering is entertainment for
Maasai as well as a cultural necessity. Dr. Erickson had
explained to us that we should bring things to trade,
like old jeans and watches, even if in disrepair.

I took my new-found treasures and went back
outside to the waiting Land Rovers. Squeezing in
between Darsi and Dr. Erickson, I showed them what I
had just acquired. Darsi, being experienced and having
an eye for this sort of thing, spoke first as he took the
bracelet out of my hand.

"What is this?" He looked at it in the sunlight
from the window. "Ahh, that's bloody ivory, I bet," he
said. At first, it didn't resonate with me.

"What? Really?" Ivory had never crossed my mind. To me, it looked like it was carved from a big femur bone.

"Yah. You know, ivory has been illegal here since 1975. But it is hard to tell." He examined it again. "Only under a microscope can you be sure. Hmmm." Dr. Erickson agreed.

"Well," I said, "what should I do?"

Darsi thought for a moment and then said, "If anyone asks, just say it is pre-ban. Your grandmother gave it to you. The rings are definitely bone though."

The bracelet was about one inch thick all the way around; it felt heavy and smooth on my wrist, and looked buttery and rich against my pale skin. Now I had something tangible to remind me of Africa. The whole experience left me feeling as if I had reconnected with something old and familiar, like a long lost friend, but one I'd never met.

Maybe I felt that way because I had been dreaming of Africa for almost a decade. Maybe it was because, somewhere between the green hills and verdant valleys, the pines, and the pond of my childhood farm, I imagined myself in other wild places. Big places, like Africa. Perhaps the idea came to me while chasing butterflies in our alfalfa fields or playing archeologist. Maybe it was while gazing out my bedroom window at the beautiful mimosa tree that lived there. This tree was so different from all the other trees, I often wondered why it was here. I loved to climb it so I could see the hummingbirds and the bees that went from one spiky pink flower to the next, gathering the sticky nectar. Dressed in fernlike leaves, thorns, and puffy pink blooms, it virtually buzzed with life! And its broad flat canopy made it exotic compared to all the other trees in my backyard. Or, maybe my desire to go to Africa had sprung from the pages of my many wildlife books, or from the National Geographic magazines my family subscribed to. However it happened, I was drawn to the Dark Continent, and always would be. So in 1983, when I stepped onto that grass landing strip in Nairobi, Kenya in late June, it felt *right*.

But my story of Africa really began with my early connection to nature. In 1966, when I was two years old, my parents bought a farm in a rural part of Baltimore County, Maryland. In truth, 3423 Blackrock Road was a run-down log cabin turned Victorian farmhouse, circa 1780. It sat in the middle of a thirty- acre valley surrounded by almost three hundred acres of farmland my grandfather bought at the same time. The outbuildings were choked with briars, and the weedy lawn hid the beautiful curves of an otherwise idyllic setting. But my mother and father saw something more. They had a vision of restoring it to its original glory—a colonial home complete with all its log outbuildings and its massive chestnut bank barn. It was the better part of a decade before a sweet white house with black shutters emerged onto four sweeping acres. The bank barn was refurbished, and a new lake was built, fed by our own little spring that ran through our yard. Then a manicured lawn with ornamental trees and themed gardens emerged. Like a huge lush jade canvas, it was accented with retaining walls, stone steps and terraces, rock gardens, and even a traditional Japanese pond and garden. Our lawn was framed by fields that my parents leased to dairy, corn, and soybeans farmers. The land beyond that was left to grow wild. The engineer and architect in my dad, and the artist in my mother, raised destruction and construction to an art form. In the end, it would be their masterwork.

My first memories of the farm were of the seasons, how they transformed the land and the beauty each one brought. Whether the valleys were frosted with ice or aglow from an August sunset, this enchanting place filled my heart. I still remember how the morning mist held the valley for a time before giving way to bright blue skies and billowing clouds. I loved to watch the day melt into night, only to begin the dance all over again the next morning. I could hear pheasant's calling, foxes howling, and owls hooting, all reverberating through the valley, soothing me to sleep.

I remember summers filled with endless seas of grass, and fields of flowers and butterflies. Fall was the time for wood cutting and the smell of wood smoke as fireplaces crackled with flames throughout the house. In winter, snow that covered the nearly mile-long driveway and water in the buckets froze, so that the ice had to be broken so horses could drink. Spring brought renewal, as apple blossoms, spring peepers, toads, baby birds, and barn swallows returned.

I loved when the barn swallows arrived! For me, they have always been synonymous with home. Beautiful to watch, they seemed to be everywhere. Lined up on the fences, watching us from the electric wires, swooping over the pond for insects and in the barn rafters, you couldn't mistake their cheerful little squeaks.

From the beginning, I was in close proximity to animals. By age four, my main job in life was to allow forty domestically-raised mallards to fight to clamber up onto my lap or get as close to me as they could. Every day at 4 o'clock, I would go into our utility room and get an old metal Chock Full o' Nuts can, scoop out cracked corn from a bin, toddle out by our springhouse, and call the ducks for feeding time. I sat down on the grass with my can in my lap, and the ducks would just overwhelm me. I loved it!

It wasn't much later that my knack for drawing started to really blossom. At first, it was just pencil drawings of various subjects. But when my mother bought me a dime-store pallet of watercolors at age ten, I became completely absorbed in capturing animals on paper. It was at that point that my mother decided art lessons would help me, and they did. For two summers, my mother took me to a private instructor who taught me everything she knew about painting wildlife and how to master watercolors. By the end of those two summers, I understood how to capture the glint in an animal's eye, the feel of fur, color mixing, and most of all, the illusion of light. Long, cool shadows up against warm bright hues fooled the eye into thinking there was light coming from a source that wasn't there at all.

From then on, I painted whenever I could. Around this time, I also became an avid bird watcher and butterfly collector. There was an amazing variety of birds tucked away in the background of my home. So, in between school and the chores on the farm, I was either watching wildlife or painting it. Saturday mornings before breakfast and Sunday afternoons after church, I saved for painting. It didn't matter whether it was a songbird or an African lion, painting nature from photographs was a joy for me. And when I got stuck, I turned my art and my photos upside down to let my right brain sort things out. This was in 1976, before Roger Sperry had discovered that we even had two hemispheres, much less how to shift from the left hemisphere to the right. Soon, people were asking me to paint for them. By 1978, at age fourteen, I was commissioned to do several fox paintings at $400. dollars each.

As time went on, my days unraveled in mostly carefree ways. With Nature as my muse, I was continually discovering, exploring, and examining the rustic beauty of my world, and the farm provided the perfect venue for just that. There was a rich combination of colors and textures—the golden hay fields, the bright red tractors, and the iridescent feathers of the barn swallows as they sat on the fences, the charm of weathered wood, rusty buckets, bright white paint on rough surfaces, and well-used farm tools. The charm was in the details, and in their history. In return, their stories became part of my paintings and part of my story.

As I grew older, my wonderful home remained an endless well of ideas and inspiration, especially the eighty-acre forest that overlooked our valley. Dense with beautiful black pines and undergrowth, it was easy to get lost in its tangled depths. In the middle of it, these trees harbored a secret treasure, rare and enchanting—wild pink orchids. There were hundreds of these flowers known as Pink Lady Slippers. A signal to spring, they brought a mystical quality as they magically appeared practically overnight, bloomed for only a short while, and then were gone.

At the heart of the forest, the scent of decaying pinewood and pine needles always reminded me of Christmas. I would sit out there for hours. The sun shone through the canopy of the trees and dappled light all around me, like gilded dewdrops. Illuminated in this cathedral of trees, I felt close to the Source.

And so the wild places became a haven, a place to listen to the deafening quietness of the towering trees and the low whispers of the zephyrs that blew through

the needles. Their soft but powerful words echoed
through the woods and deep within me. So much so,
that at seventeen I wrote, 'The Pines and I.'

I feel a spiritual oneness with these pines,
They have their unique existence and I have mine.
Yet they are linked with me and linked with Mother Earth,
So we become one merged spirit, bound from birth.

Our hearts are in the same place, wherever we are,
Joining our loving spirits no matter how far.
Together standing anchored by roots of some kind,
To this earth, to this land; heart, soul, body and mind.

Although our spirits are divided and alone,
The pines by bark and wood and mine by skin and bone.

Finding The Fire Within

Our souls rise above us, no longer protected,
When nature moves us and our spirits are affected.

Like the balmy, warm wind whispering to our souls,
Our spirits are tempted to come out of their molds.
Easily the breeze sends them skyward, swiftly blown,
Swirling up, destined to merge together, unknown.

Emotions join us to the rich soil at our feet,
Lending us a lasting comfort, our souls complete.
Creating one spirit of our adoration,
A patriotic love which has duration.

When grasping this clean, dark warmness in my hand,
I feel proud to be alive and breathe on this land.
Again I experience my quickening heart,
Reminded of my love for this wood, nature's art.

The pines' spirits are in my blood, part of my life,
And this part will live on through happiness and strife.
Even after our structures have returned to dust,
Our nourished love will melt into the earth - a must...

For future evergreens to live and grow on,
So loyalty to this land will never be gone.
This love causing our spirits to join together,
Creating one being- existing forever.

Finding The Fire Within

What mattered to me was art and nature, and both came from something much bigger than me, something that held the cycle of birth and death, fluid and endless. Not surprisingly, reading had also become part of who I was, and who I was becoming.

My mother always said she liked my hair short, so that is the way I wore it. Add in my trim, strong build and dirty blonde hair, and people described me as a "tomboy." For some reason, I wasn't afraid to do tomboyish things. I climbed trees and ran through the woods like an Indian with my Shetland Sheepdog, Dash. I played scientist, digging up old bones of unlucky animals who had perished by falling into one of the window wells around our house. Any snake, rabbit or chipmunk that found their way in usually couldn't escape the slippery metal sides and died there. I reconstructed their skeletons by numbering the bones. For me, it became a giant puzzle to then put them back together.

I never wanted for something to do. Nature was my playground and when something caught my eye, I either painted it or wrote about it. So, in 1981, when my mother discovered a trip to East Africa through a local university, I leaped at the chance! Africa, where not only the living animals were abundant but so were the dead.

The zoology department had an annual trip to the Republic of Kenya. My opportunity would come in the summer of 1983. It was a safari, camping on the ground, to study the animals up close in the wild. I was elated!

The only hitch? Money. I had to come up with as much cash as possible to meet the $4,000. price tag. My parents said they would match whatever I made. I got to work painting portraits of horses and dogs commissioned by our neighbors and friends, and started saving money. And so, my journey began.

CHAPTER TWO
Nairobi ~ The Journey Begins

"All our dreams can come true,
if we have the courage to pursue them."
~ Walt Disney ~

As life rolled on, I kept practicing and
experimenting with art, exercising that part of my brain,
and gaining more and more visual acuity. On the other
hand, school was less interesting, and B'-s and C'-s
seemed to be my destiny. High school math concepts
eluded me and my math career ended with Algebra II. I
wasn't sorry to see it go.

However, my art sales were going so well that I
began to think of art as a career, and thought of
enrolling in college just part-time. After I graduated
high school in the spring of 1982, I enrolled in
Advanced Photography for a semester at another local
school—Villa Julie College. By the fall, I was elbow-

Finding The Fire Within

deep in the guts of animals of all kinds that we were dissecting in my zoology class at Towson University.

The class, the zoology department, and the safari were all headed up by professor Dr. Howard Erickson. He was not new to the experience of taking students to East Africa; he had done it for a dozen years and he knew his way around. We would be camping under the stars every night for three and a half weeks. In fact, there would be only three nights under a roof. On the ground, Africa could show us her wildlife, intimately and in its natural state. Sometimes on foot, without electricity, running water, and communication, our tents and sleeping bags would be our most luxurious creature comforts. To me, it sounded like heaven.

By spring of 1983, I started preparing in earnest. I purchased a Canon A-1 camera with some telephoto lenses and did a little research on the parks and the places we might see. In the era before computers and smart phones, easy access to foreign newspapers and such was confined to the library.

Everything was on track until January 1983. Suddenly, the dream was threatened. In what should have been a routine wisdom tooth extraction, something went terribly wrong. Instead of the swelling going down over the next couple of days, it was getting worse, and I was in more pain with every day that passed. My parents were alarmed and kept calling the doctor. He said I would be fine. He never explored the possibility of a staph infection but that is exactly what I had. My jaw-bones and face were in unimaginable pain, pain that even double pain medication wouldn't help. By day eleven, the swelling had rendered me unrecognizable, my jaw had frozen shut and my throat was beginning to close. I could feel my life slipping away.

My mother took me to the emergency room, and the stares I received from the nurses was unsettling, to say the least. Suddenly, I was the object of pity and amazement. Before they would even admit me, I had to be placed in the care of a highly competent facial reconstruction surgeon. Dr. Donald Lurie had learned his craft by rebuilding faces of returning Vietnam vets, so it was my lucky day. Dr. Lurie took one look at me, and without any show of emotion, set to work. He took pliers to pry open my jaws, which had swollen shut. He contemplated the infection. It was so close to breaking the skin along my jawbone that he considered cutting me from ear to ear to let it drain. He gave me one of the strongest antibiotics available at the time to knock out the bacteria, and sent me home.

It took weeks of hot and cold compresses to get the swelling down, and I did slowly recover. I retreated into the pines to heal and absorbed myself in art, hoping to find my old self again. The trees couldn't see me, and it allowed me to refocus on life again and the beauty of living.

In my childhood, I had lived through many accidents. When I was nine, my pony kicked me in the temple and knocked me out cold, leaving me in a field. The doctors were amazed that the pony hadn't cracked my temporal bones – which could have killed me easily – but the bruising lasted months. Shortly after that, I watched in horror as my dad fell off a horse, landing on his back and fracturing it. He barely missed being paralyzed, and was in a back brace and on bed rest for six months. When I was ten, I fell through the barn floor into the stall below. Surprised but fine, there were no after effects. And there were other scary moments, but the staph had brought me closest to the edge of darkness, and it would cast the longest shadow of uncertainty so far.

Dr. Lurie had saved my life that day, and my face, but he wasn't able to save my confidence completely. I went into Africa with a bruised ego and a new sense that the world was unstable. Hindsight being our clearest vision, it was the perfect set-up.

In the meantime, June 1983 was fast approaching. I turned my attention to the several viruses and diseases that mosquitoes and stagnant water could bring us in the tropics. Because I was now a student of zoology, I knew of all the dangerous pathogens and parasites I would be facing in East Africa. For malaria, I took two kinds of quinine pills for three months prior to leaving, and continued taking them during the trip and for three months after coming back. Inoculations against yellow fever, cholera, typhus, and hepatitis A and B were a must. However, I would be exposed to even more than that.

No one mentioned being in good physical shape for this trip, but between all the farm chores, riding my bike, riding our ponies, swimming in our pond, and the sports offered in high school, I imagined my level of fitness would be adequate, despite my recent illness.

As the days grew longer and spring came to the farm, my safari to Kenya drew closer, becoming more real with every passing day. As promised, my parents matched the money I had earned and now there was nothing to do but wait. Time couldn't move fast enough. And yet, there was still a lot I did not know about this trip and about Kenya.

One day, my dad said to me, "Heather, you know who you should call?"

"Who?"

"My old friend George Small. George and I met when I was in my early twenties. We were on an expedition in Canada. We were canoeing across and carrying the canoes over land in between."

"Really? That sounds exciting!"

"George is a great guy, and he inherited a big ranch, 40,000 acres, in Kenya. You should give him a call. He lives right here in Baltimore."

"Oh, I don't know. I don't really have anything to say to him or ask him right now."

"Well, I have his number, when you want it," my dad said.

The truth was, I wouldn't have known what to ask him. I didn't mind going in blind, with a blank slate. The knowledge I had of the flora and fauna, the obvious diseases and the instructions from Dr. Erickson, coming from his years of travel to East Africa, were enough for me.

The main message for this trip was to only bring essentials for the bush, nothing extra. So, along with my camera and fifteen rolls of film, I packed a simple sleeping bag, my old quilt, a change of khaki clothes, the shoes on my feet, a few pairs of underwear, an extra bra, some personal items, my bathing suit, my passport, and about four hundred dollars in cash, which in 1983, was a lot of money. Most of my things fit in an army duffle bag, but I also brought along a small marigold suitcase to hold a pair of old jeans and a broken watch to trade with the Maasai.

The afternoon of June 26th, 1983, was sunny and clear. My parents, along with my younger sister, drove me to the spot in Towson where Dr. Howard Erickson and a group of about twelve other travelers were waiting.

After I got my things over to the bus, my mother gave me a hug.

Finding The Fire Within

"Bye, sweetheart. Be safe." I smiled. "Don't spend your money all in one place," she continued.

"Ok, I won't. And I'll be safe."

My dad threw in, "Have fun, kiddo!"

When I hugged my sister, the whole thing sunk in.

"Oh, Les, I'll miss you."

"Me, too," she echoed, with tears in her eyes. "Write if you can."

"I will," and I watched them return to the car. They watched as the bus pulled out on its way to New York City, where we would board the plane taking us to Kenya. We waved. Leaving the farm and my family for a foreign country was bringing up a mix of emotions. Sadness, yes, I would miss my house, my family, and my dog, Dash. But there was also a certain liberation and excitement that came with the idea of being completely on my own for the first time. As I was walking down the aisle in the bus, it dawned on me: events had been set in motion that couldn't be reversed, no matter what I did now.

On the bus, I scanned my future safari-mates. None of us had met before and I was curious about them. Our histories were all so different, and yet there must be some connecting thread. *What was it? Just Kenya? Or something more?* After all, not everyone decides to pick up and go on a trek like this—exposed, potentially dangerous, and in a land whose reputation precedes it. *What was the draw to go to the middle of the earth?* For me it was simple—the wildlife. Nothing more, nothing less; I was only interested in becoming the consummate observer and photographing the wildlife.

But there wasn't time to dwell on any of that now. Looking for a seat, I noticed that half of the passengers were under thirty, two looked around my age or maybe a little younger, and the rest were closer to my parents' age or older. One of the younger boys gave me more than a passing glance as I walked by in my bright white jeans and black polo shirt. He was friendly enough and smiled. He had darkish hair, a broad forehead, and heavy brows that framed medium brown eyes. Behind him sat another young boy, darker curlier hair with very dark eyes. He also gave me a long, hard look.

I sat across the aisle from these two as the bus pulled out of the parking lot.

"Hi, I'm Tim." the first boy eventually said. "Why are you so dressed up?"

"Well, my safari clothes are packed. And, I am not *that* dressed up, am I?"

The boy behind him just smiled and looked down.

"Where are you from?" Tim asked.

"I'm from Baltimore County. You?"

"Same. From Towson, and I have been lots of places around the world. Like Australia."

"That sounds very nice," I said.

"What about you? Where have you been?" he asked.

"Well, I've been to several states and the Caribbean, so far. By the way, my name is Heather."

"Hmm…" he responded.

The boy behind him decided to break his silence. "I'm Patrick," he said quietly. "And I'm from Carroll County. Live on a farm."

"I do, too!" I said excitedly.

"And I have been almost *nowhere*," he said with confidence and a smile.

I smiled back. "That's OK," I said. "We all can't be world travelers!"

And that is how it began between us—in paragraphs. It was a conversation that would grow with our journey, over 20,000 miles across three continents, starting with this 200-mile drive to New York. Contented, I watched the road go by out my window as we headed north on I-95. I noticed the very commercial, well-used smell of the bus; not a natural smell, nor a pleasant one. Settling in, I listened to it whine and hum as the afternoon progressed. Four hours later, we pulled into New York's JFK Airport.

As we entered one of the busiest airports in the world, I was already out of my element. After the initial security and customs check, we had a five-hour layover to wander the airport, get dinner, and window shop.

Towards midnight, I was walking by a window display of big palettes of eye shadows. I froze. It looked just like my tray of watercolors at home. *How could I miss painting already?* But in the background, I could feel Fate was fully behind me and bigger things awaited.

Our overnight flight to Amsterdam on KLM was delayed, while the entire tail section of the plane was being reconfigured to accommodate a shipment of horses en route to somewhere in Europe. The Netherlands lay nine hours away by air and was six hours ahead of New York. It would be morning again when we got there, but not even the roomy 747 granted me any more sleep. However, my excitement to get to Nairobi would prove more powerful than the lack of sleep.

I did, however, get to talk briefly to all my fellow travelers, beyond Tim and Patrick. There was Maggie, a woman in her late sixties or early seventies, who I would eventually just refer to as 'The Hardy One' because she was so resilient for her age. Alek, an aloof thirty-something man, who I never got to know. There was a married middle-aged couple, the Longs, who genuinely seemed to like each other and were from Pennsylvania. Then, there were two women in their late twenties, young at heart and never complained. The first, Lisa, would be a tent mate, on and off. And Ally, who was a friendly, open-minded and fit traveler and clearly not on her first adventure.

A grueling fifteen- hour lay-over in Holland allowed us to see the city of canals and tulips, but it would further exhaust us. Already this trip was challenging us. Even Tim and Patrick, as young as they were, looked wrung out. But exhausted or not, Amsterdam was still a delight to the eye, retaining a modern flair, while still preserving its old world charm, dressed in flowers, beautiful and clean.

The name *Netherlands* actually means *low lands,* and in fact, more than half of Holland is at sea level or slightly below. They make it all work with stone-lined canals, bridges, dikes, and levees to control the North Sea and direct the water for farming tulips and dairy cattle. Nestled between Germany and Belgium, it was possible to hear the similarities in the language, see it in the architecture, and in the people themselves. The Dutch language has a Nordic feel with Germanic undertones. The buildings were half-timbered and medieval in flavor, while the people were mostly blonde, light-eyed, fit, and well -dressed, and I caught myself staring at them.

While we had the time, Dr. Erickson also thought seeing the "red light" district might be something to do, and so we did. Because it wasn't dusk yet, we didn't see the avenues and streets lit up with red lights, illuminating pretty women in every doorway but we got the idea. We also saw the windmills and the tulips, the Holsteins, and the lush countryside. But lovely as it was, I was ready for the main attraction.

After a twelve- hour flight from Amsterdam across the Mediterranean and North Africa, the dawn light gave way to stunning clouds that were tipped in pink and salmon. The air looked clearer and the ground below was distinctly different; golden brown, open and with no lights in the early morning hours. The mighty continent of Africa loomed large as she came up to greet us. The white fluffy cloud layer gave way to bright blue skies and an ebony strip of runway in a sea of golden grass.

The landscape was like nothing I had ever seen—barren and alien, yet beautiful and appealing. I felt a chill go through my body as the powerful jet engines reversed and the landing gear was lowered. The 747 touched down onto a grass strip before it turned into a runway. *I was finally here!* Here at The Jomo Kenyatta International Airport, on the edge of Nairobi, Republic of Kenya. For years, my soul had seen the picture, and now it was real. *My God, I was here!* As the plane pulled towards the terminal, I couldn't help but notice that the airport looked out of date. I asked Dr. Erickson about it.

"Yes, well, everything here is about forty years behind. You'll see," he explained. "This airport was built in 1958. I am afraid this is where most of Africa is right now."

Forty-eight hours ago, I had left Maryland, and I was still wearing the same clothes. All of us were so tired, we were on auto-pilot getting through customs. So far, all the people we crossed paths with were so friendly.

"*Jambo*, Miss! *Habari?*" was the greeting I would hear over and over again as my eyes struggled to stay open. Thankfully, there were no delays. On our way out of the terminal into the open air, a man with a British accent walked up to us. His bounding energy almost regenerating ours.

"Hey, guys! There you are! How are you? *Jambo*, my friends, welcome to Kenya! Howard, good to see you, old chap." He slapped Dr. Erickson on the back. "How have you been? God, you guys look *tired!*"

Darsi Ruysenaar, life-long resident of Kenya, would be our guide for the next three and a half weeks. His greetings – warm, easy, friendly – exuded confidence and made it easy to trust him. His 5' 10" frame was strong and stocky. He was probably only forty years old, but Africa had taken its toll. The sun had dried his skin, bleached his hair, and toughened his exterior. His natural charm made him charismatic and a people-person through and through. His vast web of connections throughout Kenya and Europe would make our tour through Africa much easier.

"So, Howard, I am glad you made it safe and sound," Darsi said as he surveyed our crew, all the while smiling, shaking hands, and nodding. "Let's get you out of here!" He escorted us out of the airport to a small waiting fleet of Land Rovers, with some of our camp staff at the ready. Tired and drained as I was, I still noticed that the air smelled remarkably sweet and fresh and different from any other air. Perhaps it was because we were already more than a mile high, 5,400 feet above sea level.

Darsi and Dr. Erickson gathered us all together before getting us into our first safari vehicles.

"So, Howard, I have booked you all for one night at The Boulevard Hotel. I bet you won't forget last year! " Darsi laughed.

"No, no. How can I forget? Gunfire at 5 A.M. is not my idea of a wake-up call." Dr. Erickson added in his droll way.

"Well, I think you're safe this time," Darsi quipped. Tim, Patrick, and I looked at each other and then at Dr. Erickson. *What is he talking about?*

"And then tomorrow, we'll have a short time in Nairobi, then we strike out into the bush. So, enjoy your civilization while you still have it." Darsi smiled.

I already liked this guy. He had a buoyancy that was contagious. In contrast, Dr. Erickson was more cautious, older – about 50 – with curly salt and pepper hair and a simple way of being. He was more matter-of-fact and tried to keep the surprises to a minimum.

I got into a Rover with Dr. Erickson, with Darsi driving, while the rest of my safari-mates were spread out amongst the other two vehicles. While we had been talking, all our gear had been loaded onto the Rovers. We headed into downtown Nairobi, the capital city of Kenya. So far, there wasn't one thing that even vaguely reminded me of the States. In the meantime, Darsi was explaining the history of Kenya as we drove into Nairobi.

"The airport was named after the first prime minister; Jomo Kenyatta, and the equator runs through the middle, right above Mt. Kenya. To the east is the Indian Ocean, to the west are Lake Victoria and Uganda, Kenya's neighbors to the north are Sudan, Somalia, and Ethiopia, with Tanzania to the south. Basically, we are sitting on a hot bed of volcanic action here. It's a bit primitive, I know, but you should have seen it in the mid-30'-s, when my father came here!"

Finally, my eyes involuntarily fell shut. I was not noticing very much of anything as we made it to the

45

Boulevard, our promised last touch of civilization for a while. Somehow I managed to take a shower and lay my head down on a pillow before sleep overcame me. I slept for twelve delightful hours. When morning came, I felt reborn, and I took a good look at my surroundings for the first time. The room was very simple. Two twin beds with white metal headboards and a side table between. The bathroom looked circa 1950, with little black and white tile everywhere and basic fixtures. Despite the cloudy, cool day, what greeted me from the hotel window was cheery and bright—striking plants and trees, like acacias, palms, flame trees, and bright cascades of bougainvillea.

Unbeknownst to me, while we slept, Darsi was choreographing the huge production of gathering and organizing most of the supplies for our next three and a half weeks in the bush. Tents, chairs, and tables were all loaded onto an old Unimog truck, which was a four-wheel drive truck made by Mercedes after World War II for all-terrain purposes. He had also commandeered enough food, water and dry ice for the next week and had arranged for seasoned drivers, a cook, porters, and other trusted camp staff who knew the land and knew bush craft.

Wearing my safari clothes of khaki shorts, cream shirt, light gray-green jacket, and sneakers, I packed up my things and went down to meet everyone in the lobby.

"*Habari ya asubuhi,*" Darsi announced with a wide smile.

"Good morning, all!" Dr. Erickson translated. "We are going to get breakfast and walk around Nairobi while Darsi finishes his magic. Then we're back here, and then we're off. Breakfast anyone?"

Universally agreeing that we were starving, out on the street we went. I can't say I remember breakfast that day. The sights were so captivating. In the cool 60° air, we walked the sidewalks of a place that was certainly a third world country. Everything was different. The cars were driving exceedingly fast and on the left side of the road. Mostly small, foreign-built cars, that were quite capable of running you over. The native Kenyans were blacker than even in the Caribbean. The men's stares were unnerving. I hadn't expected to be looked at as though I was prey.

As we walked, Tim asked Dr. Erickson, "So, what *was* going on last year when you were woken up by gunshots?"

"Oh, well, there was a coup attempt on President Daniel Moi on August 1st last year; a group of soldiers from the Kenyan Air Force took over the radio station, Voice of Kenya, and announced that they had overthrown the government. We woke up to gunfire and a bunch of commotion on the streets. I didn't know *what* was going on! All we knew was there were orders broadcast on the Voice of Kenya to stay inside, so we did. Soon, we realized that we were temporarily held hostage in a police state. I think in the end, more than one hundred soldiers and two hundred civilians were killed."

"Here? Around this hotel?" I asked with amazement.

"Yes, they were right out here on Harry Thuku Road! And there were university students involved, and looting."

"How come, umm… we didn't know about this?" I wondered out loud.

Dr. Erickson looked at us and said, "It's over now but in countries like this, it is always a possibility. Can't let it stop you. Let's go in here." He gestured us into a shop.

He knew all the best local shops to find amazing East African crafts. The exchange rate from US dollars to the Kenyan schilling was very much in our favor, so everything was shockingly affordable, from soapstone to ebony carvings, carved salad tongs to chess sets. I was thrilled at how far my dollar went!

"Are we coming back here someday?" I asked hopefully.

"Oh, yeah, you'll have your chance to shop and get souvenirs at the end of the trip."

As we went in and out of the shops, I couldn't help but notice that everywhere you looked, there hung a picture of Moi. It seemed impossible to escape his gaze. As a visitor, it felt ominous; I wondered how it felt for the locals.

I had a chance to examine more wooden carvings and soapstone chess sets before we had to turn back to the hotel and start our journey in earnest. When we got to the Boulevard, Darsi was waiting with the three Land Rovers, our gear strapped to the roof. I hopped in the one with Darsi, and Tim and Patrick joined me in the back seat.

Through the hectic Nairobi streets, we drove at a breakneck pace, reminding me of a New York cabbie. Outside the city limits, the roads very quickly became earthen, washed out, and full of rocks and ruts. The driver slowed us down to under twenty miles an hour. As we bounced along, luggage rocking precariously on top, I started to wonder. *Were all the roads going to be like this? At this rate, how would we get anywhere?* Still, there was this overwhelming feeling of excitement.

As if reading my mind, Darsi turned around and with a big smile said, "Don't worry, guys, we'll make it. Not all the roads are going to be like this."

"Thank goodness," I said quietly.

"Most will be much worse," he finished.

CHAPTER THREE
The Rift ~ The Greatest Valley

"There is such a beauty to some; the few that capture our minds and take hostage our hearts, we are left wondering if we'll ever be the same."
~ Pete Kohlasch ~

In those first hours of discovery, on those first roads to nowhere, I realized that I was about to embark on something extraordinary and beyond my most ambitious dreams. And perhaps, in this uncharted territory, I would need more than just the wind at my back. As our vehicles started to kick up dust, the excitement was tangible as we headed northwest, Nairobi now behind us.

"So, how long have you been in Kenya?" I asked Darsi.

"I was born here, in Kitale, western Kenya. Both my parents were European immigrants. My dad left Holland in 1935 along with two friends on bicycles headed for South Africa. They knew the war was coming and Capetown was a Dutch colony. They cycled through Belgium, France and Italy, working along the way. From Brindisi, Italy they got a boat to Alexandria, Egypt and started to cycle south through The Sudd.

"The Sudd? What is that?" I asked.

"Oh, that is the swamp surrounding the Nile in southern Sudan. I don't know how they did it because it is known to impenetrable, but he somehow hitched rides on *falukas* and *dhows* down the Nile to Uganda. Right over the border is Kitale."

"Wow! That is amazing! So, why Kenya?"

"Yes, well, no one would even consider doing that trip today. Once my dad got to Kenya, he heard there was a future in coffee, tea, cattle, sisal, and more. He got a job with Lord Portsmouth running a plant nursery and coffee plantation and so he stayed. Several farm management jobs followed and so he stayed in Kenya."

"My goodness- so, you've seen the whole transformation of Kenya, from colonists to independence?"

"Indeed I have. I can't say it's been pretty. Mind you, there was the whole Mau Mau Uprising in the 1950's, when the Kikuyu and other pastorals attacked

51

the British. As far as they were concerned, when the Europeans took over the White Highlands, it was still their land!"

"Das right," said our Kenyan driver, calmly. "Dey were my people."

"Ahhh, Heather, I am sorry," Darsi said, remembering his manners. "Everyone, meet Ekevu, one of our incredible guides and drivers."

"Nice to meet you," I said, reaching over the seat and shaking his hand.

"Nice to see djou, Miss. *Jambo*." He had a big welcoming smile and a sincere warmth about him. I felt an instant connection. Tim and Patrick followed suit and introduced themselves.

"You are about to see something wonderful," Ekevu said. "*Yeye ni bonde kubwa*, she is the Great Valley." Just then, we approached a view that looked like the edge of the world. We were on the brink. *I was on the brink*.

At the precipice of the greatest valley on earth, we paused. Africa! Now she lay before me- vibrant and in living color. Looking across this vast landscape, I drank in the enormity of her horizon and the power of her great distance. As far as my soul could see, as far as my eye could be, there was nothing but wilderness.

Open, full, and without end, miles and miles of her immensity awaited. The purple ridges of the other side were discernible in the clear air, making it seem only a mile away. In fact, it was more than twenty-five miles away. On this remarkable day, I stood awestruck and in joyful suspense. It was through God's eyes with which I made her acquaintance.

"Dis *mkubwa bonde* is really a fault line. She is slowly ripping Africa apart." Ekevu began. "But she is such a beauty!" Ekevu said to all of us quietly. No one answered. We were all breathless at the sight.

"Here we go," said Ekevu, as he took our Rover over the edge. The other vehicles followed. It seemed like we should be in a free fall, so steep and treacherous the road was. It wound like a snake, back and forth, down the valley wall. There was no margin for error here, and the drivers had the challenging job of cheating disaster, staying away from the crumbling rock and dirt that would send us hurtling down the mountain. Tim, Patrick, and I looked at each other as we peered out the windows and saw how our drivers were forced to push the envelope. And yet, if you looked up and focused out across the valley, there was a kingdom of beauty and the cradle of humankind.

Even though it was the dry season on the plateau, our surroundings got increasingly lush as we descended. Acacia bushes and dry grass turned into greener and greener vegetation. Miraculously, Ekevu delivered us safely to the floor of the most striking geological feature in Africa—the Great Rift Valley. Four thousand miles long and up to thirty-seven miles wide, the Rift has cut a divide, several thousand feet deep at times, through the continent. It originates from the mouth of the Zambezi River in central Mozambique and winds north through Kenya and Somalia, ending in northern Syria, where three tectonic plates meet at the Red Sea, known as the Afar Triple Junction. Just as the nineteenth century Scottish explorer John Walter Gregory would discover, the Rift is so enormous that she dazzles the mind, opens the heart, and fills you with wonderment.

The roads were better in the valley. I knew the basic itinerary, but I was curious about what was in store for us now.

"Darsi, what's our next stop?"

"I have arranged to visit a British couple I know who live here; a private ranch. The Maasai live here, too. They have allowed them to keep their village and in return, the Maasai allow visitors to watch them perform their ritual dances."

"I'm glad I have my camera!" I said.

"De Maasai, dey do not like their picture taken, Miss Hetha. Dey believe it takes their soul away."

"Really?"

"Yeah. I'll ask the owners if we can take a few photos, though. If you ask first, they don't usually mind," Darsi admitted.

"Whoa, look at this place!" Tim exclaimed. "We are definitely not in Maryland anymore."

We all leaned forward in our seats as the relative roughness of the road ended and a carpet of emerald grass began. A testament to the fertile soil of the Rift, the lush lawn and gardens seemed to spring out of nowhere. Ekevu parked on a driveway of sorts, and we had a few minutes to explore the grounds as Darsi and Dr. Erickson met up with the owners to discuss our itinerary.

It was as if I had stepped into another world. The house was a classic African ranch house. The porch was draped in vegetation, banana palms bent over a babbling brook, while bamboo garden chairs waited in several locations. There were long sections of garden dedicated to tropical trees, most covered in canopies of vines, and bougainvillea flowers in every shade of ruby, white, and fuchsia dripping from the canopies like sparkling jewels.

The Maasai village was just a few minutes away, in the middle of an acacia grove on a dusty and well-worn part of the earth. Built in a circle, the traditional *enkaji* huts were made from small timber and branches of local wood. Built by the women, they are meticulously plastered with a mixture of mud, cow dung, urine, ashes, and grass. The *enkaji* themselves were circular in shape, and measured no more than fifteen feet across and five feet high. From the doors and single small hole in each roof, came the distinct smell of smoke from a fire that burned day and night. But it was not the wood smoke I was used to. It was a foreign and distinct smell that would become unmistakable, and that would live in the deep recesses of my memory.

Outside each hut sat one woman by the doorway. Each was dressed in a traditional beaded yoke and red *shuka* wraps, with very simple cowhide sandals on their feet. Their ear lobes were not just pierced, but wildly enlarged by big pieces of wood, or even, ironically, discarded film canisters. Even so, the Maasai's way of life and their traditional herding of cattle and goats had remained unchanged for many centuries.

Instinctively, we all gathered on the perimeter of a clearing and waited. The light became strangely bright, even though the sky was cloudy. In my heightened state of anticipation, the colors seemed amazingly vivid, the air wonderfully clean, and the smells which surrounded me keenly distinct.

I heard them before I could see them — a deep, guttural buzz in the distance. And then, out of nowhere, came powerful warriors, spears in hand. They hopped in unison, alternating feet, one behind the other. Highly decorated and in their war garb, their voices became an instrument, hypnotic and haunting. A chill went through me. Defying description, it was an ancient and primitive growl. It seemed the percussion of life, the universal beat, heartbeat, drumbeat, hoof beat. Underneath their voices was the hum of the earth. I watched, entranced by their fluid movements, as they moved as one. One being, one heart, one song. It was so raw; a forgotten part of humanity that I had never seen before and didn't know if I would ever see again.

The warriors continued their dance as they transitioned into a new phase. Still chanting in rhythm, *Ooooo-yah-, Oooo-yah-,* along with a low growl and staccato cough, they faced us in a semi-circle. I noticed that their legs were decorated with what seemed a random pattern of light gray "paint." One or two wore the menacing, traditional oblong black ostrich feather headdress, framing the face, as they showed off their jumping skills. All had braided hair, plaits mixed with red oxide earth and animal fat, giving their long locks a crimson undertone. Wearing bright red loin cloths, they jumped in pairs, each seeming to try to jump higher than the pair before them had. Heels never touching the ground, bodies straight, their nimble feet left the ground. Seeming to hang in the air, light as a feather, the beads that lay across their chests bounced with them. This was the *adumu* dance. In Maa, this simply means, "to jump up and down in dance."

Eventually, they reorganized into a line and turned to bring the dance to a close. They hopped away, taking the unforgettable sound of their voices with them. So evocative, this would remain deep in the recesses of my mind, their chanting lingering. For me, this would become the rhythm of Africa.

Our drivers were waiting patiently. As I climbed back in the Land Rover, the spell was broken. Tim, Patrick, and I shared a back seat again. As we drove on, out of the corner of my eye, I caught Patrick looking at me.

"Turn onto the road to Naivasha and Nakuru," Dr. Erickson said to Ekevu.

"Dat is northwest, *mheshimiwa...*"

"Right. We are headed to Lake Baringo, and then Lake Borgoria."

"The lakes here along the floor of the Rift Valley are all volcanic in some way," Dr. Erickson explained, as he turned towards us in the back seat. "The volcanic soda ash coming from within the earth makes most of the lakes alkaline, with a few acceptations. Baringo is one of only two fresh water lakes. It has a fresh water source from three rivers—the El Molo, the Perkerra, and the Ol Arabel. The water has no visible outlet, no place to go."

"So, de water goes home, back to de earth, through small fault lines," Ekevu finished.

"Do you guys like bird watching?"

"Sure!" we all said at once.

"You can't help but do that where I live," Patrick said. "On our farm, they are everywhere."

"Chickens don't count," Tim teased. He laughed and I had to smile. Patrick threw him a look.

"I take my camera or binoculars into the woods at home all the time," I said looking at the boys. "Does that count?"

"OK, you three. Anyway, Baringo is known for the bird life; probably close to four hundred species there. And Borgoria... well, you'll see."

The truth was, up until now, our itinerary seemed built around travel. I was glad for a chance to test my bird-watching skills and my new camera. Let the safari begin!

"We will be driving through some rich farmland," Dr. Erickson said. "It's the perfect altitude and rainfall for growing coffee."

"I thought I had heard that," I said. "I love coffee."

"Yah, Nakuru and Bungoma for sure," said Ekevu, naming two coffee valleys. "But really, over dat way, in de high plateaus of Mt. Kenya, dat is where good coffee lives." He pointed to his right. "Dey have thousands of farms growing mostly, and it is mostly my people still," he added with a smile.

I wondered out loud, "Will we get to see some coffee up close?"

"I'm afraid not. No, not this time, guys. But maybe you can take some Kenyan AA home, though."

We passed by Lake Naivasha and the national park built around it. On our right loomed the Aberdare Mountains, which create the eastern boundary of the Rift. After going through the town of Nakuru, we continued north on the road simply known as the Road to Nakuru. That's when we saw them. In the distance were acres and acres of lush coffee farms, covering hills that never seemed to end. Thousands of acres of red berries that loved the cool altitude at night, ripened in the equator's sun by day, ready to be harvested, and then sold to be enjoyed by millions.

As the road unfolded northwards, home and everything familiar seemed a lifetime away now. I wondered what was ahead. One thing was for sure, in this place that grew and sold superior coffee to the world, I would have to wait until I got back to America to taste it.

CHAPTER FOUR

Moto Maziwa - Water from Fire

"Some say the world will end in fire, some say in ice."
~ Robert Frost ~

About thirty-five miles south of Lake Baringo, we crossed the equator for the first time. It was simply marked by a yellow sign that would become familiar to us in our travels. Lying just ahead, between the Laikipia Escarpment and the Turgen Hills, lived Lake Baringo. She was 50 square miles of vibrant waters, at 3,200 feet above sea level.

The roads were better here, paved, and as the scenery went flowing by, so did the trappings of my former life. As it would be most days, the roof was open in the Land Rover. Taking full advantage, I stood up, head and shoulders towards the sky. The wind played in my hair and pushed the clean air into my lungs. I took deep breaths. A sweet sense of freedom started to take hold, the kind that you feel only occasionally. Time was suspended, recent memory forgotten, and everything that I was and had been was no longer significant.

Without a watch, I did not have a good feel for how long it took before we turned down a dusty driveway. The sign said "The Lake Baringo Club." *Yes!* We were here! The driveway transformed into a beautiful flat area, and a pristine lawn stretched out before us. Again, we were welcomed by prolific palms and a dozen groupings of bamboo chairs and tables. Surrounding the lawn perimeter was a hand-stacked stone wall about three feet high, draped here and there with red and pink bougainvillea. Acacia, papyrus, and flame trees also dotted the bright green grass. To our left, we could make out wide stone steps leading to the pool, also invitingly surrounded by lush floral vegetation.

We all got out and began to explore the grounds. There were misty, purple, rolling hills visible in the distance, across the very still waters of Lake Baringo. At first, there was nothing special about this water. It was brackish and brown with reeds and grasses that looked remarkably like the ones back home. Then I looked closer. There were signs saying, "Caution. Hippos and Crocodiles are dangerous." *What?* Hidden in the murky brown water were giant things I couldn't see? I took a few steps back. This was not like back home. There we had snapping turtles that hid in the muddy depths of our pond, but this was a horse of a different color. I knew that human attacks were not uncommon, and were usually quite serious.

I scanned the lake. Unbeknownst to me, there was another deadly enemy living out there, and all around us. Unseen. Quiet. Stealthy. Even in their great numbers, we would not be able to see these disease-carriers until it was too late.

With my camera, I was able to very quickly see the birdlife Dr. Erickson had spoken of. There were little grebes floating in groups, White egrets skimming the water, and a Goliath heron standing like a statue in the reeds. Walking around the shoreline, I spotted some beautiful kingfishers wearing iridescent patches of turquoise and purple. Under the trees, the tweets and twitters of birds were surrounding me with exotic songs only the equator could dish out. Looking up into the acacias, there were Little Bee-eaters, a Red- billed Hornbill, and a White- crowned Coucal, birds I had only seen in books! The sound of their calls became the backdrop to the beginnings of a marvelous afternoon.

Back on the lawn, we all sat and rested in the bamboo chairs as the sun began to fall slowly lower. A comforting and sweet tiredness was coming over me. Apparently, we would camp next door at a place called Roberts Camp, known locally as *Kampi ya Samaki*. We walked over and watched as our camp staff set up our tents. It was a pleasant piece of ground to camp on and it still gave us a view of the lake. In fact, some tents were erected rather close to the water's edge. I wondered whether they had read the signs.

On the equator, the sun drops suddenly out of the sky at six o'clock every day and reappears exactly twelve hours later. Ekevu and the other drivers gathered wood for a fire. As the fire took hold and lit up the night, the temperature started to drop quickly. Darkness brought a stark contrast to the bright day—it dropped to 45º. Our campfire became critical for heat as well as light. Huddled around the fire, the feeling of adventure was almost palpable amongst our party of travelers. It felt real for the first time and full of opportunity.

Our cook and Ekevu had prepared a meal that was surprisingly involved for the bush. I would be continually amazed at their dedication to our well-being, from setting up the latrine tent everywhere we went, to meals, snacks, laundry, everything we needed to be comfortable.

After dinner, we talked around the campfire, as we would do every night.

" 'I have two hands!' That is what my father said, trying to convince my mother's father to approve their engagement," Darsi said to us, smiling. "When he saw the size of my dad's hands, my grandfather was immediately won over!"

"How did they meet?" I enquired.

"Back then, there were ads in the British papers encouraging people to colonize East Africa and so my mum's family came to Kenya in 1935 as well. My dad, Jan, met my mother at a Sunday social in 1936, with all the other Continentals. They got married in 1941, and in the end, he and my mother farmed 4,000 to 5,000 acres, with 2,000 head of Boran cattle, five acres of coffee, and 1,000 acres of maize. I still wonder how they did it."

"What happened to the farm?" asked Tim.

"Well, in one of Kenya's many land grabs, my family was evicted, basically, off their land. 1973 was one of the worst years for the White Highlands."

"How can they do that?" interjected Patrick." In the United States, nothing like that could happen!"

"Oh, but it already has," said Dr. Erickson. "We also have a history of land grabbing. Just look at the American Indians. Not to mention the land grab of the Oklahoma territory in 1893."

"Even recently, during Kenyatta rule, they're taking land along the coast, like in Mombasa!" Darsi's indignation was quite evident. "But, my parents ended up being one of the top three breeders of Boran cattle in all of Kenya by the 1940's and my father was decorated by the queen for his services to the crown."

"That is impressive." I said. Everyone else agreed.

I looked at Ekevu. He remained silent, but I sensed a depth and a passion about him just below the surface. He smiled when I glanced over, and when the others retired to their tents, I stayed at the campfire a little longer.

"*Memsahib*, djou might tink about sleep. Another day comes tomorrow."

"Oh, I know," I sighed. "Goodnight."

"*Usiku mwema*, Miss."

"What?"

"Good night. And be sure to zip de tent closed, Miss, or de mosquitoes will take a bite!" Ekevu grinned. I smiled back.

As I snuggled in my sleeping bag that night, my ears started adapting to the foreign and mysterious noises. This night, it was the song of the cicadas, some birds, and an owl. *Was that a grunt from a hippo?* Would the crocodiles emerge from the water tonight? Or maybe a hippo? What would we see tomorrow? Eventually, my tired body must have overtaken my mind because I drifted off to sleep.

The dawn brought a sunrise reflected in the lake and smells of food cooking over the fire. The scent of cinnamon and other spices, which I did not recognize, were carried in the air. I got up and made my way over to the fire. The cook was stirring a fragrant liquid in a pot and the aromatic steam surrounded me.

"Good morning, Heather," Darsi said. "Sleep well?"

"Yes, soundly, too. I was surprised."

"How about you guys?" he said, turning to the others, who stood warming themselves by the boiling pot. "Did you all hear what happened last night?" We all looked at him and shook our heads.

"Well, some hippos came up to graze last night and they thought poking their heads into a few tents was a good idea. Luckily, that was all they did. No one got hurt. Maybe a little shaken. The hippos, I mean."

"Oh, are you kidding?" I said.

"No, it's true," said Dr. Erickson, as he walked over. "But keep in mind, the Cape buffalo kills more humans than any other large mammal here."

"That's comforting," I heard Tim say under his breath.

"I thought you were a world traveler?" remarked Patrick. "Not up for the adventure?"

"Oh, I'm ready!"

"Does anyone want to try some chai?" broke in Ekevu. "Made with real goat's milk, my friends... Miss Hetha?"

"Yes, please," I responded, knowing nothing of chai. Made the traditional African way, it was hot and comforting, and included loose Kenyan tea, cardamom, cinnamon, and raw sugar. It was the East African version of our basic tea. *Oh, what a treat!*

"Anyone else?" Ekevu ladled out chai until it was gone. As for the rest of breakfast, we had fresh goat's milk butter on homemade bread, as well as some staples like eggs and bacon. Everything tasted better than it did back home. After breakfast, we walked to the water's edge, smooth and still in the early morning light.

Darsi said, "Now, guys, look out for the old tortoises here. They are very used to people and they will let you touch them."

"How old?" asked Tim.

"How old, Howard, are these turtles?" Darsi asked.

"Oh, about one hundred, some of them," Dr. Erickson replied. "And after we finish with breakfast, we are going to take a morning tour of Baringo, do some bird watching. And later, we have an unusual stop to make."

"Who wants to see some snakes?" Darsi asked. At home, that would not be an ice-breaker, but in Africa, it made sense. To be able to see the most poisonous snakes here before we got into the bush was brilliant!

"We want to take you to Jonathan Leakey's farm to see some snakes so you know what to look out for," Dr. Erickson explained.

"I used to pick up snakes all the time back home," I said. "Black snakes and garter snakes mostly, but they still had a bite! I remember one time I got bitten by a big black snake as I was trying to pick him up behind the head. He got me in the crook of the opposite hand, between my thumb and forefinger. I bled for an hour!"

"Exactly!" said Darsi. "But these snakes won't give you a chance to bleed. Some of the bites from these cheeky chaps are considered unsurvivable!"

"What do you mean, *unsurvivable?*" Patrick said quietly.

"Dead in, well, just a few steps. We call them 'the three step snakes'," Darsi said, as he turned and walked back to the main camp area. "I'll see you guys when you are ready for the morning game run."

We all looked at each other and at Dr. Erickson. "The idea is to not get too close," he said, and turned to go with Darsi.

"He is right." Ekevu told us solemnly. "De Black Mamba, she will give djou de kiss of death. Dey are de *Walinzi wa Pazia* - Keepers of de Veil."

This was the first time I had heard of a mere translucent piece of fabric keeping life from becoming death. We all are dependent on the veil to keep us safe. Whether you describe it as sheer luck or destiny, we are all just visitors, hoping for strong fibers, especially in Africa.

"Meet me at de vehicles." Ekevu's voice was so expressive and lilting, it was like a melody.

I suppose Tim, Patrick, and I were drawn to Ekevu's happy nature. Without thinking about it, we would always opt to drive with him when possible. Pulling out of the Baringo Club's driveway on our first real exploration of the flora and fauna in the tropics, the equatorial sun penetrated the morning chill and made everything warm again. We drove around the perimeter of the lake, stopping once in a while to take photos, absorbing a place that practically sparkled with brilliance. The birds and butterflies were so brightly colored, they dazzled the eye and lifted the spirit. There was such abundance! Everywhere you looked, there was evidence of Nature's elegant design.

I asked Dr. Erickson, who was in the front with Ekevu, "So, do we have any anti-venom if we get bitten by any of these…snakes?"

"Uh, well, I am not sure. It's so expensive and it needs to be refrigerated at all times. I would hope Darsi has access to some."

"Where is this snake farm?" Tim asked.

"It's right near here. Right, Ekevu?"

"Yes, sir."

"Jonathan Leakey's place should be coming up here soon, on de…"

"Jonathan Leakey! Any relation to Louis Leakey?"

"Oldest son," replied Dr. Erickson.

"Who is Louis Leakey?" Tim asked. "I have never heard of the guy!" I looked at him and Patrick.

"Oh, seriously? Olduvai Gorge? The famous archeologist who discovered the oldest human remains?" I was having trouble believing they had never heard of him, but they just shook their heads.

"In the early 1960s, he found a huge cache of fossils, right here in the Rift. It was big news at the time," I added.

"Still is, *Memsahib*, and Louis was close to de Kikuyu. In fact, dey considered him a Kikuyu."

"Very interesting. I didn't know that."

Patrick turned to me on the backseat and asked, "How do you know so much?"

"I used to watch National Geographic, and read. Plus, I am sure in school we were taught about the Leakeys. Somewhere."

We pulled onto a dusty driveway that led to a dusty open area dotted with some rundown buildings. Darsi hopped out of one of the other vehicles and went to look for Jonathan, or any sign of life. He came back shortly with some native snake handlers, safety sticks at the ready.

"Gather 'round, everyone," Darsi said. "We are about to see some snakes that you don't want to meet out in the bush. Pay close attention."

He turned to one of the snake handlers, "*Ambapo ni,* Jonathan?"

"*Yeye si hapa,*" was the answer.

"OK, looks like we can't find Jonathan, so let's begin. *Kwenda mbele-kupata nyoka baadhi,*" Darsi said to one of the staff, and they left to go into one of the buildings.

"Instead of following in his dad's footsteps, Jonathan decided to raise snakes to sell and export to zoos, harvest venom for the anti-venom serums, etc."

Just then, one of the snake handlers appeared carrying a Black Mamba. We all watched the snake twist its body, trying to free itself from the noose of the safety stick secured around its neck. This was not a snake you would want to meet in the dense sugar cane fields or underneath a coffee plant. And yet, that is exactly the danger Kenyan agricultural workers faced every day.

"So, tell us more about this Black Mamba," Darsi said to the handler.

"Dis snake, he is de fastest and most aggressive snake in de world. Djou cannot outrun de Black Mamba! Dey can move at up to twelve miles an hour. And if dey bite djou, you have less than twenty minutes to live."

"Tell them why they are called the Black Mamba," Darsi suggested.

"Oh, it is because de inside of de mouth is black, not their skin."

Dr. Erickson added, "And aren't they the longest poisonous snake in Africa?"

"Djes, djes dey are..."

Next, a few more handlers came out, one with a King Cobra and one with a Green Mamba; both deadly, but not as toxic as the one we'd just been shown. We learned that the Green Mamba is not as aggressive, but still highly dangerous. King Cobras were also a concern, but it was the well-camouflaged pit vipers, that were the color of rocks and earth, we needed to be sure we saw before they saw us. *So, what our chances were of running into one of these snakes?* I asked Darsi if we were going to have access to anti-venom out there.

"No, I am afraid not, dear girl." Darsi said. "Too expensive and highly perishable to take into the bush, plus it has to be administered on the spot, otherwise it isn't effective."

"So, how do people survive out here?" I wondered out loud, trying to keep up with him as he walked towards the vehicles.

"They don't," he replied as a matter of fact.

When we returned to camp before lunch, I couldn't help but notice we were all starting to gather dust. My simple white T-shirt was blotted with it, and when I greeted Ekevu, his bright white shirt, now unbuttoned halfway down his chest, was not bright white anymore. I imagined that my short blonde hair was now on its way to being truly dirty blonde, and askew, if it wasn't already.

As I walked through camp, I heard several of the staff, who were standing together, talking in Swahili and then watching me closely. The phrase I kept hearing was *matiti ni nzuri sana*. I glanced back over my shoulder and by their reaction, I seemed to be the object of their conversation. It was quite unsettling, so I asked Dr. Erickson what they might be saying.

He translated, "I think they are saying you have very beautiful breasts."

"What?" I exclaimed. "No! Are they? *Really?*"

"That is what *matiti* means. Sorry."

"OK. Thanks, I guess." Now I was truly unsettled.

I walked over to the fire where the cook was, as did Ekevu and a few others, including Tim and Patrick. As he approached, Tim was laughing. He and Patrick stood on either side of me.

"Hungry?" Ekevu asked. We all nodded.

"I am, for sure," said Tim enthusiastically. Then he leaned in and whispered in my ear, "You do, you know."

"What are you talking about?"

"You know, you have nice breasts."

"Oh, gosh, *what?* How do you know?"

"I have eyes. And I heard what Dr. Erickson said." Tim was all smiles. I rolled my eyes and gave him a look. I hoped no one else heard us.

After lunch, we all collapsed into a chair or went back to the Baringo Club and sat under an acacia or a palm, depending on our mood. On our way back, after whiling away the afternoon, the path revealed the ancient reptiles Darsi had spoken about several days earlier. Moving at the rate of the continental drift, these creatures looked like they from another age. With the top of their shells reaching as high as thirty inches above the ground and about five feet from end to end, it was easy to see why they were called giant tortoises. It was too rare, so I hopped on the back of one and rode around for a while, though we didn't travel very far.

As the sun dropped out of the sky again and the chill came back into the air, we moved towards the campfire. Ekevu stoked it into a roar. The light brought us in, closer and closer. On chairs or the ground, we sat in quiet bliss and watched the flames lick the cool air. Now, out here in the bush, we could almost tangibly feel that intangible thing that made this experience so delicious and unique. In the open air of Africa, we had the moon over head, warm food in our stomachs, and the fragrance of wood smoke all around us.

"Dinner was lovely again. Well done, everyone!" Darsi raised his glass to Ekevu and the cook staff.

"Yes, thank you all, for this." Dr. Erickson
added. *"Asante."*

"So, get a good night's sleep, everyone. We
leave for Lake Borgoria in the morning, and then onto
Amboseli for a few days."

Sleep came easily, and in the morning, after
breakfast with chai, we packed our things and headed
down the driveway of the Baringo Club. Turning south,
we backtracked through the Rift to this much smaller,
shallow saline lake. I was with another driver this time,
but still sitting in the back seat with Tim and Patrick.
We opened up the roof and stood up for a while until
the morning air got too cold. Then we were content to
watch from inside the Rover as the landscape change
from lush to progressively more and more barren. Soon,
there was a new feel to the air. It was moister, and with
a whiff of sulfur. In the distance, we could detect a
glassy surface, but it was not until we got right up next
to Borgoria that we could appreciate her true nature.

Reflected in the smooth surface was such a
precise mirror image the cool blues and greens of the
Siracho Escarpment that I had to look closely to see the
distinction between it and the reflection. Then smell of
sulfur in the breeze was inescapable. The Rovers parked
and we got out and approached the edge.

On foot, we could feel the warm, moist air
rising. From deep inside the earth, even in the heat of
the day, the vapors plumed and traveled the lake's

surface like a fluid ghosts. Around the edge were pools and other openings from which boiling water bubbled, then exploded into giant geysers, spewing hot water high into the air. Like Pele, the Hawaiian goddess of fire, this volcanic lake screamed of white hot power.

Standing next to a boiling pool, I felt the heat, and the danger. A hapless person or animal that fell in would be boiled alive. Dr. Erickson was careful to make sure we did not get too close to the slippery rocks that lined the boiling pools.

In the distance, there was a mass moving across the surface of the lake. To the naked eye, it looked like pink icing skimming the vertical line of the lake. Floating and fluid, it was slowly moving so I used my zoom lens to investigate. To my surprise, the mass was hundreds of thousands of pink flamingos! So beautiful, as they marched and swayed in unison, slowly and methodically sifting through the caustic waters for algae. The minerals of the lake supported this food supply, which sustained the masses of flamingos. It was here, not Lake Nakuru, where they chose to breed, nest, and raise their young.

Suddenly, something alarmed them and they took flight. Instantly everyone turned their attention to a sky. Awash in pink, the ascending cascade of a million wing beats produced a mighty roar, a thunderous crescendo. I couldn't take my eyes off this deafening and thrilling sight nor could anyone else. We lingered, watching the pink sky until it dissipated and storing up all the sensation we could out of this enchanting place, born of fire and baptized by boiling water. You could practically feel creation under your feet. Darsi, Dr. Erickson, and the staff hung in the background, waiting for us. Then Darsi called everyone back to the Rovers.

"Come on, let's not dally, we're waiting," he said in his jovial manner. "Say good-bye to Borgoria, and the Rift. I want to get to Amboseli by afternoon."

Darsi drove this time and Ekevu sat in the passenger's seat. Our convoy of Rovers and supply truck headed south, crossing over the equator again and passing the Aberdare Mountains on our left. It would take a couple of hours to reach Amboseli, which brushed the border of Tanzania.

Ekevu turned around in the front seat with his most engaging smile and said, "Are you ready for Kilimanjaro, Miss Hetha?"

"Yes!" I said, smiling. "I'm excited to see it."

"Wonderful. I am excited to show it to djou, Miss Hetha."

CHAPTER FIVE
Amboseli ~ The Shadow of a Legend

"The woman who follows the crowd will usually go no further than the crowd. The woman who walks alone is likely to find herself in places no one has ever been before."
~ Albert Einstein ~

Our trilogy of Land Rovers flew through the Meshanani Gate on the north side of Amboseli National Park, then we slowed to a stop, a new ashen dust swirling energetically around our vehicles. We parked in a wooded area with mostly fever trees. Their eerie yellow bark stood out against the dark undergrowth.

"Why are we stopped?" I asked.

"Shhhh," whispered Ekevu. He rolled down the window.

"If we are lucky, we may see some giraffe," Darsi whispered. "Roll down your windows."

I looked around as Tim and Patrick slowly rolled their windows down. There was no movement yet, so we waited.

"Ekevu has a knack for this, guys," said Darsi, quietly.

"Shhh…I think I hear something." Ekevu put his forefinger to his lips.

The trees themselves seemed to move as, out of nowhere, three Maasai giraffes glided into view. Their jagged brown spots had disguised them among the shadows of the acacia leaves. Watching them move with such a graceful yet lumbering gait made their height seem even more remarkable. Just one hundred feet away, they stopped and looked right at us. It was a juvenile and two adults. With my telephoto lens, I could see their big eyes, fuzzy horns, beautiful sloping necks, and impossibly long legs. *Could it be? Here I was, with the tallest animal on earth?*

"Hetha, and you too, boys, if you stand up slowly and open de roof, djou might get a photo."

Luckily, they weren't easily spooked and we caught a good glimpse of them before they turned and blended back into the fever and acacia trees. It was so easy for them to become part of the bush once again. This ability to fool the eye with false shadows was a brilliant way to disappear. Later, I would understand that in Africa, it was the only way.

Finding The Fire Within

Ekevu drove us out of the woods on faint roads that turned into even fainter paths. Now, sitting on the roof, we had a better view of the widening savannah. The triple peaks of Kilimanjaro; Shira, Kibo, and Mawenzi, came into view. Zebras and wildebeest scattered as we approached the legendary volcano.

"Ahhh, there she is!"Darsi said.

"Ohhhhh,"was all we could say. Forgetting to breathe, I tried to absorb the magnitude of this giant volcano, and wondered how Hemmingway and all the other explorers reacted to her towering presence. Her once-fiery breath, now icy, the volcano loomed in front of us. In the warm light of the fading day, I gazed at her renowned slopes, appearing amethyst with shadows of indigo. The snow blowing off the frigid cone was so bright white it looked neon. Acacias dotted the base on a broad canvas of dusty gold and ochre, seeming to anchor this ancient volcano to the ground. The zebras and wildebeest that had scattered from us had gathered in the foreground and were joined by Thompson's gazelles, all swishing their tails vigorously to keep flies away. They looked happy and peaceful, and stopped to look at us before continuing their dusty march.

"Kilimanjaro is really in Tanzania," Darsi said. "But as you can see, it casts a long shadow. It is the highest summit in Africa."

In the shadow of the legend, we just absorbed her splendor. I knew even then that no photograph or painting could really capture her magic, but that wouldn't stop me from trying.

As we turned around, the volcanic dust billowed up behind us. Ekevu told us to keep our eyes peeled for wildlife. Soon, animals started to pop up that I had only seen in books! A pair of impalas walking in the brush, herds of zebras braying and kicking up their heels, warthogs running with tails held high, and vervet monkeys playing on the ground. A pair of zebras, lit up by the sun, paused to investigate us, and I took the opportunity to snap a picture.

"Do we have a place to camp?" Darsi asked Ekevu.

"Yes, *bwana. Hakuna wasiwasi, mimi yote figured nje.*"

"*Dalili yoyote ya majangili?*" inquired Darsi.

"Not yet." Ekevu responded.

"What are they saying?" Patrick whispered to me.

I shrugged. I only knew a few words in Swahili and I hadn't heard any of them just then. Ekevu pointed to a sparse grove of trees and Darsi gave a nod. So we carved out our first real bush camp under the sprawling branches of the acacias. Getting our gear off the big supply truck would always be a chore. Today, Tim asked me if I needed help picking a spot for my tent.

"Oh, thanks, I'm fine."

Patrick watched me scout for a good place. One of the staff came over with a tent and set it up for me. Where would we be without them! According to Dr. Erickson, we had time for one quick game run before nightfall, when lions hunt. On the equator, night comes swiftly, so we needed to be alert.

Dr. Erickson opened the door of a Rover for me. A driver I hadn't met yet – Lucas – was at the wheel. Pulling out with the windows down, we could feel the chill in the air. Driving on paths that barely existed, I wondered how our guides could find their way in this immense savannah. And how would they find our way back? The sun was low in the sky. The Amboseli plain was alive with creatures that we hadn't seen so far —

Finding The Fire Within

Olive baboons and vervet monkeys that observed us with darting glances. Their bright, intelligent eyes followed us as we passed. It was hard to tell if we were watching them or they were watching us. We also passed some waterbucks resting on the ground and impalas grazing in the last rays of light.

"Do you think we can find some lions, somewhere close?" Dr. Erickson asked Lucas.

"Djes, I know where dey like to be."

Sure enough, after searching for about half an hour, we came upon a pride of lions lounging on a dry patch of earth. They seemed in no particular rush, and looked well-fed and content, and certainly not afraid of us. These powerful hunters were amazing to see so close. I looked at their fur, their eyes, watched their tails twitch and the mouthful of teeth when they yawned.

"It's getting late," Dr. Erickson said to Lucas. "Let's go back." So Lucas turned the Rover around.

Once we neared camp, threads of fragrant smoke carried on the evening breeze greeted us. Our cooks had been preparing a simple Kenyan bush stew, and the delicious aroma of cooking meat was in the air.

Ekevu announced, "Come. Come and sit by the fire." To stave off the night's chill, we gathered 'round. He turned to some of the staff. "*Kwenda kupata baadhi ya zaidi ya kuni.*"

Soon, they brought more pieces of dead wood to toss on the fire. The dry acacia and fig branches made the flames pop and sizzle, flaring up and releasing sparks into the air, floating upward until they burned out.

The first sounds of twilight were always the cicadas and crickets, followed by the baboons calling. Finally, in the distance, a lion's roar penetrated the air and a hush fell over the camp. Dusk turned to night and I savored my dinner, all the while looking deeply into the darkness. I am sure we were all thinking the same thing. *What animals and snakes were out there? Would they come near tonight?* Beyond our ring of light, nothing was discernible, just inky blackness.

The camp staff was already asleep nearby, since they regularly rose by 5 A.M. One by one, my fellow travelers left the campfire and retired for the night. Then Darsi and Dr. Erickson soon followed, saying *kwa-heri.* I stayed by the warmth of the fire until it was just me and Ekevu. I was tired too, but I wanted to enjoy the tranquility just a little longer.

"Djou like dis fire, Miss Hetha?" Ekevu stated more than asked.

"I do. It reminds me of being home. Summer nights just like this, clear and bright, and the smell of wood smoke. My dad would take my sister and me to the top of one of our hills. We could see the stars and the whole place. We'd sit and make a fire where the cows had cropped the grass close to the ground, roast marshmallows, watch the fireflies, and just be."

"Dat sounds lovely," Ekevu said smiling, "and peaceful."

"It was," I said, staring into the flames. Suddenly, I missed home terribly.

"But here dis fire is more than heat," Ekevu pointed across the leaping flames, "because out there are de animals."

"So, the fire keeps the animals away?" I asked hopefully.

"Mostly, djes. But djou can see de eyes before dey get too close. Fire lights de eyes!" he said, pointing to his own eyes with two fingers.

"Oh!" I looked around me. No bright spots in the darkness yet. Ekevu smiled one of his big smiles. His warmth was infectious.

"Djou might get some sleep, *Memsahib*. A fresh day comes tomorrow."

"Yes. Thanks, for dinner and, well, all of this."

"Djou are very welcome, Miss Hetha."

"See you in the A.M.," I smiled and went out beyond the ring of light.

"Wait, Miss, it's too dark. Dis night is not used to djou." He picked up one of our few kerosene lanterns and walked ahead of me, through dark, to my tent.

"*Kwa-heri.*"

"Goodnight," I said, and slipped inside. Tucked into my sleeping bag, I stared at the ceiling, processing all the things I had seen so far. I thought of home, but more than that, I hoped the fire would burn bright and keep us safe. At least for tonight.

I was awakened by the sounds and smells of breakfast. My fresh chai and goat's milk awaited me! Even back home, this was my favorite time of day. The anticipation of new surprises and new possibilities always excited me. This morning, eggs, bacon, and toast were on the menu. Everything we ate needed to be non-perishable or found in the bush, like fresh fruit and bush meat.

As I was eating my eggs, out of the corner of my eye, I caught Tim looking at me. He was smiling. I smiled back. Still smiling, he asked, "So, what are you doin' out *here*, darlin'?"

"Same as you," I said, "looking for adventure."

"Really?" He replied with his heavy eyebrows raised.

"The truth is, I'm here to take photos of the wildlife for my art, *and* for the experience."

""Hmmmm… I guess that does make you different from all the other girls I've met. And I've been to lots of places."

"I'm just doing what I love. Different or not, I am afraid this is the real me."

"Well, I noticed you right away on the bus. White jeans, black polo…you stood out." He winked.

"I hope in a good way?" I said, flirting.

"Of course. But I think the white jeans might have been a little optimistic for out here."

"I see that now." I replied with a smile.

"So, what kind of art do you do?"

"I paint in watercolors mostly. Animals, birds...nature, really, and pets." I said.

"Wow, that's cool! You're lucky to have such a talent."

"Actually, I am lucky to be able to paint at all."

"What do you mean?"

"See these?" I held out my arms, palms up, and showed him two long scars in the crooks of my elbows.

"Whoa! What happened to you?"

"I was flying down a hill on my bike one day, going down a path between our farm and the farm next door, where I always go, and the farmer had put up a new electric wire fence. I didn't see it and the wire caught me right here, on my tendons. Then, because of the momentum, the wire slid up to my collarbones near my neck, then it snapped. I pulled down three locust posts. Meanwhile, I had to push my bike home. The cuts were deep enough that the doctor said I was lucky that it didn't cut my tendons that move my fingers."

"Wow...I...*man*, that must of hurt." he said. "You *are* lucky."

"I know!" As every day, I threw back my malaria tablets and washed them down with water. Suddenly his expression turned serious.

"What?" I inquired.

Looking distracted, he abruptly got up and took his plate back towards the cooks. *What was that about?* I looked around and there was Patrick across the table, watching. Quietly, from a few chairs down, he smiled.

"Why was he so…"

"I have no idea," Patrick cut in. "But, it looks like it's time to get ready for our morning game run."

He stopped and looked right at me. I smiled back and paused. He seemed to have more to say.

Finally, I said, "We better go." He nodded reluctantly. We all knew the drill. When the drivers gathered around the Rovers, it was time to wrap up breakfast and pick a car. Today, Tim and Ekevu were standing by one Rover, along with Dr. Erickson and a few others. Ekevu opened the door for me and then started to get in the driver's seat.

But before he could, Darsi came over and announced, "Hey, bro, I'd like to drive today, show Howard something."

"Be my guest, sir," Ekevu responded, opening the door for him.

I saw Patrick waiting by another Rover, hand on the door, looking at me. His glance was intense. I waved and got in quickly, just as Darsi was starting the engine.

Today, Amboseli was slightly gray, clouds hiding the sun, which was only going to punctuate what Darsi had in mind to show us. Within Amboseli were many micro-ecosystems, including lush areas with low-growing palms, marsh land, plains, and acacia groves. We were headed somewhere unique, and that somewhere was like nowhere. Looking like a war zone, the landscape in front of us was filled with the dying. Fallen acacias with their bark stripped from the trunks and the foliage stripped from the branches, dead and bleached from the sun, looking like bones.

"What happened here?"

"Elephant damage," Darsi said, "When they run out of food during the dry season, they turn to what they can find—the trees and the underbrush." He pointed over his steering wheel.

"Wow." I muttered.

"This is why some people think it is OK to kill elephants, poach them. Somehow, they rationalize it's saving the trees," Dr. Erickson explained. "But really, it isn't necessary to kill elephants. Natural selection works."

Just then, two male waterbucks walked into view. They were the only signs of life in this otherwise desolate expanse. Then, about fifty yards away, two juvenile bull elephants began sparring and throwing gray dust into the air. Darsi explained that if these were adult bulls, we might have seen a serious contest, even blood.

The Land Rovers could only go so deep into this wasteland. Fallen trees would let us go no further, so Darsi backed up and turned around.

"Now where?" Tim asked.

"Howard? What do you want to scout for?" Darsi asked.

"Let's see if we can find a herd of elephants. What about the more lush grasses near the marshes?"

"You got it."

Dr. Erickson had a keen knowledge of habitat from past trips, and Darsi had the experience and navigational skills to get us there. Like a puzzle or a riddle, you never knew what to expect in the bush, so every day, every minute, was charged with anticipation.

Soon, wildlife started to appear; a Crowned Crane hunting for small reptiles close to the marshes, a Cape buffalo lying on the ground, surrounded by Great Egrets hoping for a meal of insects. Baboons and vervets played by the side of the road, and a Maribou Stork, looking shockingly ugly, stood by, waiting for the remains of a kill. Then we saw them.

Lumbering out of the mixed brush came a small herd of elephants. As these gray giants casually made their way towards us, Darsi stopped and turned off the engine. We watched as a tiny new calf appeared from under its mother. Darsi decided to creep a bit closer. *How close were they going to get?* We soon got our answer

—*really close!* Only twenty feet away, the baby was so adorable with his big eyes and long lashes, his tiny trunk and wobbly gait. In person, you realize how enormous these animals are and how, if they wanted to, they could really ruin your day. Weighing eight tons or more, it would have been easy for them to use their size to intimidate, but they didn't. Gentle and social by nature, they seemed at home with us, and occasionally raised their trunks into the air to check our scent. Eventually, after we got some great pictures, they passed us by. Flapping their ears and making low grumblings, they retreated to the dense greenery they had emerged from.

"They are such magnificent creatures," said Darsi. "Let's go see some friends of mine."

Hidden in an acacia grove was a very small block building. Outside stood a few uniformed men, presumably park rangers. As we pulled up, they marched confidently forward. It wasn't until Darsi hopped out and greeted them that they relaxed.

"Hey, bro! *Jambo. Habari?*" is how he addressed them, and they in return. Warmly shaking hands, they talked, and eventually motioned us out of the Rover. The one driven by Ekevu arrived next with Patrick and a few more of our crew. Darsi chatted with the rangers in Swahili, no doubt getting caught up on any recent activity in the park.

"Guys, look at this." Darsi took us over to a collection of tusks lying on the ground. One of the rangers hoisted a tusk and stood it on end while Darsi picked up another tusk. Before I knew it, I was standing between 120 pounds of ivory. Holding the tusks, one in each hand, I supported them by myself! They were not only heavier than me, but taller. To a Kenyan, they would be worth over $6,000. One by one, we all got a chance to stand between the tusks, and photos were taken for posterity.

"Dis ivory comes from elephants dat have died naturally, but we also have seized dem from de poachers," one of the rangers informed us.

"*Je,ni katika kumwaga?*" Darsi asked one of the rangers. "*Mitego, umwagaji damu mitego tumepata,*"came the response.

"Djou can take a look if you like," the ranger said with his arm outstretched towards the building.

Darsi motioned to us to come with him, and Ekevu and I followed him. Inside the small ranger's station, the only light was from the open door. The dirt floor was only about ten feet square. Not much room for anything except what was piled up in the corner—a stack of snarled wire.

"What...*are they?*" I asked.

"See dis?" Ekevu reached out and touched them. "Dey are wire snares. Animals get caught and dey slowly die of starvation or exhaustion from strugglin'."

"Most likely for elephant," Darsi added as he stepped back out into the daylight.

I looked at the circles of wire, covered with dried blood. *Oh, my God...*

I looked at Ekevu. "I know how wire cuts."

"What do djou mean?"

I faced the light and showed him what the wire fence had done to my arms. He reached out and tenderly held my elbows. A furrow came over his brow.

"My *gosh*. I am glad djou are alright."

"Mmmm, me too."

He extended his arm towards the door, so we went back outside and rejoined the group. Before we got back into the Rovers, I asked, "What happens to all the tusks?"

Everyone turned their heads to look at me. The ranger looked me up and down, pausing on my bracelet. Darsi quickly answered in his British accent, "I'll... I'll tell you...what. Why don't we all say good-bye? Time to go."

Dr. Erickson chimed in, "Yes, let's head back."

They both shook the rangers' hands, then herded us all towards the Rovers. Tim and I got in and looked at each other. Darsi got back in the driver's seat and sped off, as much as you can speed off in the bush.

Back on bumpy roads, I was lost in thought, watching the scenery go by and thinking about the poor animals caught in those snares. Closer to camp, we passed some zebras and wildebeest, and an eagle in a dead acacia, looking regal and vigilant.

Then, out of nowhere Ekevu said, "Stop!"

Darsi skid to a halt. "What is it, bro?"

First Ekevu hopped out, then Darsi, who motioned to us to stay in the Rover. There on the ground, to the left vehicles, was a swarming, undulating mass.

"OK, come on out," Darsi said. "Just don't get too close."

Quickly and silently moving nearer, we saw that the mass was ants, tumbling over each other in a massive trail that was eighteen inches across, and black with a reddish iridescence. I had never seen *anything* like it.

"Watch out, back up," Darsi said, as Tim and I inched closer.

"*Ndiy*, dis is *marabunta*," Ekevu added, "Dis is not a good way to die."

"Die?" Tim exclaimed.

"Yah. Dey are driver ants, and if djou get in their way, dey will bite djou to death."

Good Lord. We all took a giant step back, but I was able to take a picture before we got back in the Rover.

Arriving back in camp, we saw Dr. Erickson and his driver Lucas, along with Patrick and the others who were already there, talking excitedly amongst themselves. When I walked over to see what was happening, I noticed Patrick looked a bit shaken.

"What's going on?" I asked. Lucas lit up.

"We were in dis elephant herd, *Memsahib*, and dis big bull elephant came over to our Rover. He leaned on our car and pushed us with his trunk and his body. Oh, did he rock us!"

Ekevu laughed.

"Yeah," Dr. Erickson added. "He did give us quite a ride there, but we are all fine."

Patrick was rolling his eyes. "It depends on how you define that." he grumbled. I laughed.

"Oh, but guess what we saw?" Tim announced. "Marabunta!"

"Wow! Really?" said Dr. Erickson, "I bet that opened your eyes."

Darsi slapped Patrick on the back and smiled, turning to walk away, "See! All in a days' work, my boy."

At lunch, Patrick and I ended up sitting together and out of earshot of the others. All of us were much browner than when we began, and on Patrick, it complimented his dark eyes and curly hair. As a teenager, in these conditions, he had remained remarkably composed.

He asked, "So, what high school did you go to?"

"I went to a St. Paul's." He looked puzzled.

"It is a private school."

"Oh," I heard the tone change. "Why not the public high school, like Hereford High?"

"I'm not sure," I said. "My parents came from a private school background and I guess they thought it would be better for me to be in a college prep environment." Patrick nodded. "But, I guess *that* didn't pan out because I'm out here!" We both laughed.

"And I was the only one in my class who didn't go to college full-time!" I said with a laugh. "I don't think my school liked that." He chuckled, too.

"Well, I'm in the high school in Carroll County, and then I work the farm on the weekends."

"I'm in touch with that! We take care of three hundred acres where I live. It's hard work and it never seems to end."

"I know," he said smiling.

"Every June, we join forces with our neighbors to bale alfalfa hay, and it is always ridiculously hot. And it doesn't take long before our shirts are soaked and the hay sticks to you as it comes out of the baler." He nodded his head in understanding.

"And then we have to unload it and toss it up to the top rafters in the barn, where it is even hotter!"

"Oh, I've been there!" he exclaimed. Then, his look softened. "Are you dating anyone?" he asked quietly.

"Mmmm, no, not right now."

"Really? That is hard to believe," he said
sweetly.

"Why?"

"Because you're pretty and, I don't know,
smart."

"I am not sure about the pretty part. Have you
looked at me lately?" I glanced down to my dusty arms
and dirty shirt.

"OK, well maybe not as pretty out here," he
responded with a wide smile.

Eventually, Darsi came over to check on us.
"How are we doin' here?"

"Fine," we said.

"Later, Ekevu tells me we are going to make a
point of looking for some big cats. I know leopard is out
there, but they are hard to find. Most likely we'll see
lion. Sound good? OK, see you guys at 4 o'clock sharp."

"Alright," we nodded.

On our game run that afternoon, and for the
next two days, we were lucky enough to see the lions of
Amboseli. Lying in small groups, they are easily found.
We'd pull up beside them and marvel at their
handsome looks and sheer size. Content and naturally
confident, they were spectacular to see in their natural
environment. They let us observe them without
incident. They never got up to leave, and we were able
to take our time to absorb them. The cubs were so
carefree and playful, the mothers were patient, and the

males were gentle and protective. We took a snapshot of their world, yet we came away with so much more. Free and happy, that is the way I'll remember them, and how I hope they will remain.

Each magnificent day in Amboseli led to an even more magnificent one. From the first giraffe to the herds of wildebeests creating billowing dust, to the secretary birds, the impalas, the baboons, and even the vultures, it felt like the kingdom was intact and vital. Even though there were bigger parks ahead, greater expanses, and maybe grander adventure, Amboseli was my first experience with enormous open spaces and was providing a new and humbling view of life.

As we gathered around the campfire after dinner one last time before moving to the next camp, I could feel the electricity in the air, the anticipation of what was next.

"Maasai Mara tomorrow, guys," Darsi announced. "Part of the original Maasailand. Should be the place where we see the most wildlife so far."

Now one week in, we all were settling into a new way of living. Without ceilings or floors, there was no place to hide. For me, somewhere between the starscape and the landscape, the sky and the dust, God and the ground, a new perspective was taking shape, one without limits. And even though I was a tiny thread in this huge, vibrant tapestry, I was beginning to understand my part in it.

Finding The Fire Within

The next morning, we all had to rise extra early to help pack our tents and our things so that we could leave promptly after breakfast. Ekevu came to my tent with a lantern in hand.

"*Memsahib*, time to get up. We want to see your shining face before de sun's today," he said softly.

Within the hour, the Rovers were assembled in a convoy, along with the supply truck, ready to go. Ekevu opened the door for us once again, then slid into the front seat. Darsi was going from vehicle to vehicle, doing a spot check and head count. He stuck his head in the passenger window.

"Got everything we need, my man? Good, fine job. Let's hit the trail." He was off to the next truck before Ekevu could even answer. There was a long pause before Ekevu slowly turned around to look at me in the back seat.

"What djou call those guys in your country? Cow-men, cattle- ...?"

"Oh, you mean *cowboys*?"

"Djes, dat's it!" He chuckled. "Dat's him. What djou tink?" I laughed out loud.

Just then our convoy started to move forward, so I stood up and opened the roof for the best view. I looked back to take it all in one last time before the sweet hours spent there were just a memory. I would remember her well, sleeping in the shadow of a legend.

Now, we were hurtling towards our next grand experience amidst six hundred square miles of savannah, umbrella acacia, and mixed brush. This *mtoto wa asili mama*, a child of Mother Nature, awaited our arrival and held within her borders all the power that Africa had to offer. In the park, three mighty rivers would collide and join forces—the Mara, the Talek, and the Sand rivers, all bringing essential water to a place that pulsates with life around the clock. Like nowhere else on earth, the Mara would show us a constant dialogue between birth and death, and in a way that everyone understood. From here, the real safari began, and our road ahead was about to get a little rougher.

CHAPTER SIX

The Mara ~ The Vast Grasslands

"All I have seen teaches me to trust the Creator
for all I have not seen."
~ Ralph Waldo Emerson ~

As we headed southeast, Ekevu stopped briefly
at the Ololaimutick Gate at the border of the Maasai
Mara and said something in Swahili to the ranger. We
had somehow gotten far ahead of the rest of the caravan
and were leading the way towards our campsite. The
faint path we followed led to a panoramic view. The
savannah was so immense, it stretched the imagination.

Venturing into the Mara on this insatiable
summer day was like walking into a masterpiece, a
canvas prepared with deliberate and loving hands. The
sprawling savannah grasses were carefully painted
with a mixture of vibrant olive greens and yellow
ochres, and were punctuated by purple cloud shadows.
The open sky was awash in cobalt and cerulean blues,

providing a backdrop for big fluffy clouds. In the distance, low hills were stippled with dusty blue. Acacias, which sprung up randomly, gave it pattern. Paths carved by millions of hooves drew me into the landscape with undulating curves, while the grasses gave it texture. The breezes that swept them, sending the grasses into a swaying dance, gave the Mara movement. And finally, the massive waves of wildebeests, zebras, and gazelles crisscrossing the plains gave it life.

God, the sheer size of this place! If I were painting it, how would I capture the light I was seeing? What colors would I use? Where would I start?

Predominately green, the Mara was still in a period of growth and abundance from the rainy season. She had many darker shades, but for now, her green grasses were high and lush. This attracted birds and breeding animals in an endless drama that never stopped unfolding.

We stopped on a small crest to survey the scene. With the windows down, fresh air filling our lungs, and with the sun shining all around us, Ekevu and I took in the dreamy beauty of this wild landscape. As we stood still, it was all around us—a life force that overwhelmed the senses. I could hear it, smell it, taste it. The grunts of wildebeests, the brays of zebras, and a dozen other noises blended together into one. On the breeze was the taste of sweet air mixed with a distinct accent of earth.

Ekevu and I just gazed at the canvas before us; it seemed suspended in time. *Such splendor!* Finally, he broke the silence. Out of the corner of my eye, I saw him smiling a knowing, contented smile.

"*Kwa sababu ya kunyesha mvue. Alitupa zawandi.*"

I turned to look at him, and he translated, "Thanks to de rain, she gave us gifts." I smiled back. *Oh, such amazing gifts!*

Before we started the Rover's engine again, Ekevu pointed out a clump of trees far in the distance.

"See dat?" he asked.

"Just barely," I said, squinting and leaning forward. I got out my camera and, with a zoom lens, took a closer look.

"Dat is de Talek River, Miss Hetha."

"OK, I see some dark green trees in a line…"

"Well, you keep an eye on dat," he smiled.

He ground the stick shift of the Rover into gear and we began our journey towards the Talek. We rolled along a path of just two faint tire treads pointing towards a cluster of rounded trees that gripped the river. It seemed an oasis resting upon a sea of wheat-colored grass. The river, which wound through the park like a serpent, sometimes turned back on herself before stretching out again to meet the Mara River. Draining from the highlands, the Talek depended on the rains feeding her so she, in return, could feed the land and the wildlife.

There was so much to look at, so much to absorb! I tried to take in the colors, textures, and subtle tones of these massive grasslands. We passed delicate Thompson's gazelles swishing their short tails; bat-eared foxes congregated in small packs around their den, ears huge and alert. I saw warthogs, Olive baboons, and Cape Hunting dogs. I still hadn't seen a cheetah or a leopard. I hoped the Mara would expose one of hers, just so we could catch a glimpse. As we approached the Talek, my excitement was rising.

"We are almost there," Ekevu announced enthusiastically. Coming closer, the setting was delightfully idyllic and romantic. Like something you might have read about in a book, it was a haven of giant fig trees nestled on the water's edge. The trees hugged the riverbank and threw a blanket of much needed shade on the short, golden grass. Their canopies gave it a feeling of security and privacy, making it seem like a perfect site to set up camp.

Ekevu stopped on the threshold of the grove and got out to survey its possibilities. Hands on his hips, he gave it a thorough looking over. Then he left the parked Rover there so the others would see it.

"Dey will come soon," he said. "Djou can go. Go and explore, if djou like," he said to me. "I will be right here."

Standing by the river's edge, I peered over its bank. It fell sharply to the water below, which was about ten feet lower than its level in the rainy season. Once overflowing with the seasonal rains, you could see where the rushing torrents had eaten away at her banks. The brownish water only meandered now. As the dry season progressed, the river bed would become more exposed and eventually become a dry basin, only to repeat the whole process with the onset of the next rainy season.

Next to me stood fig trees adorned with bark that looked like our sycamore trees back home. The bark of both trees grew lighter with age, shedding their darker tones. The figs were like old women, graying on top near the canopy, which gave way to dark greens, browns, and grays lower down the trunk. In the large forked trunks, vervet monkeys chattered as they sprang from branch to branch. They were not far off the ground, so I got a good look at their little black faces, fuzzy grey fur, and darting eyes. So cute, I wanted to take one home. I watched them for a while until I heard the sound of engines.

Unloading was always a time of bustling activity and anticipation. Ekevu was giving directions to the staff as they set up. There was always something to do and they paid attention to every detail.

In short order, Tim and Patrick came over to see what I was looking at.

"What's goin' on?" Tim asked me.

"Oh, just looking around."

"Beautiful spot," Patrick added thoughtfully. It was great to just linger in such a lovely setting. From the shadows of the trees we got a real appreciation for what went into our camp sites. The rhythm of Swahili voices bouncing through the air was comforting. The rattle of all the equipment; the tents getting erected, the lanterns being hung here and there, scattered chairs unfolded and organized, and duffle bags being deposited neatly in front of each person's tent. And finally, the fire came to life, always a welcome and comforting sight and sound. Then, the sound of cooking pots washed, and the table being set for lunch. Tim said what we were all thinking.

"Where would we be without these drivers and porters?"

"We would be, well, nowhere. Literally, nowhere." I said.

"We'd be at the mercy of this God-forsaken bush country," Tim said.

"It is not God-forsaken," was my response.

"OK, maybe not God-forsaken, but forsaken anyway. We just wouldn't survive without them." Tim coughed a deep, dry cough. "I'm going to go find some water and go to my tent and lie down."

Patrick looked at me and shrugged his shoulders.

"I am feeling a little parched myself. Can I get you some water?" Patrick asked.

"Absolutely."

Walking back, we stepped through shadows under the figs trees. In camp, we could see that the midday meal was being prepared and that Darsi was engaged in a conversation in Swahili with a few drivers. They were pointing here and there and talking excitedly. No doubt plans were being made to go on our first game run into the Mara after lunch.

Patrick went to get me the water and I stood looking out over the plains. In the distance, I heard the faint tinkling of metal. Soon, it became a jangling and a clanking. It sounded like cow bells. *Cow bells?* I walked out beyond the edge of our camp, beyond the trees, to the precipice of the endless plains to scan the horizon. Finally I saw them. Coming towards me from my left

was a moving mirage. As they approached, I could see
red *shukas*, bright and bold, among cows and goats.
They had shaved heads and wore heavy beaded yokes.
Mostly women, I guessed. They slowly made their way
towards our camp. Maybe they had heard our vehicles,
or seen our tire trails, or maybe it was just by chance
that they were passing by. Nonetheless, the Maasai kept
coming.

Up close, I could see that these women were
pierced and adorned with jewelry. Even as dusty and
thin as they were, they were smiling. Without words, I
felt a connection. We were mutually curious. A blonde
white woman out here was still somewhat rare. I smiled
back and said *jambo*. They chattered in Swahili. One
woman approached me and touched my arm, and then
my hair.

It was hard to imagine women constantly on the
edge of starvation could support life, but they did.
Several of the women had babies with them, tied up in
fabric slings on their backs. They also brought with
them that signature smell of sour goat milk, cow dung,
and dust. Fascinated, I observed them as they turned
and kept marching west, fading into the landscape.

The Maasai had existed out here for centuries.
They lived a simple life, and survived by harmonizing
with the land, and using the blood, meat, and milk of
their livestock. They followed Nature's lead beautifully
in an ancient dance of respect.

So why did I feel this sense of sadness? Maybe
because of a misplaced belief that I could provide
something that was missing in their lives, something
that they needed. In truth, they were in need of nothing.
In fact, the next time I would encounter Maasai women,
I would be the one in need.

Still thinking about the women, I wandered
back to camp. It was humbling to see the Maasai
women's sense of joy in the face of constant struggle for
survival. But I was beginning to get it—the struggle was
not necessarily to keep from dying, but to keep living,
despite the circumstances here.

Patrick was waiting with my water. "What
happened to you?" he asked.

"Oh, I got involved with the Maasai! Did you
see them?"

"I am afraid not."

"I wish I could have taken a picture of them.
They were so interesting!"

"You know they don't like that."

"Yes. I know. Still..."

"Lunch is ready, Heather. Let's eat."

"Alright!"

After lunch we listened intently to Darsi and Dr.
Erickson, who were in a discussion about logistics as
well as the current state of the wildlife populations here
in the park.

"How many Black rhino do you think are left now, Dar?" Dr. Erickson asked.

"Oooo, there bloody well better be the five males I counted a few weeks ago! And maybe fifteen total?"

"Hmmm, only five males left. Well, at least we haven't lost any since I was here last."

"Still, that's pathetic, Howard. Five males? There used to be nearly one hundred individuals in this park, just ten years ago." Ekevu walked over.

"Dr. Howard, de poaching is gettin' bad. But my friends, I heard dat dey are putting surveillance on de rhinos here now."

"Right. He's right, Howard. So I hope that begins to stop the slaughter."

"Dar, if we are lucky, could we find some of those males today?" Dr. Erickson asked.

"I don't see why not. Ekevu, what do you think?"

"I tink if djou take de one road towards the Oloololo Escarpment, dey might cross your path."

"OK, well, you've heard it here first, folks. Let's get ready to move out." Darsi stood up and put his hat back on. "Sun is hot today. Drink some water, guys." He went to find Lucas.

Tim didn't come out of his tent until the meal was being cleaned up and everyone was boarding the Rovers. I was a little concerned about him, but he managed to join us for our early afternoon tour. The drivers were ready and we were anxious to explore these vast grasslands for the first time. I grabbed my camera and hopped into the back seat of a Rover with Darsi, and Dr. Erickson and Patrick jumped in with me. There was no room for poor Tim, and he didn't look happy about it, either! Ekevu stayed behind to help the camp staff set up and prepare dinner. He waved as we pulled away.

Once we got out in the open, the ground was fairly smooth and level. We were able to speed across the Mara, rolling along faster than we had yet. The wind blew in through the open windows onto my face, my hair blowing, and the afternoon light radiated everywhere. The savannah was highlighted in warm yellows and heightened by lengthening plum shadows. Everything had a romantic glow.

It was in this lovely afternoon light that we came upon the Oloololo Escarpment. It held miles of long, flat-topped hills, dotted with acacia scrub. In the foreground, antelopes perched on small mounds of dirt. They looked as if they were the gate-keepers. I leaned forward in my seat.

"Are these Topi antelope?" I guessed.

"Quite!" Darsi replied. "Good guess. How did you know that?"

"I suppose all that research I did before we got here paid off," I smiled. Patrick smiled too.

"And do you know what they are standing on?" he asked Patrick.

"I haven't the faintest," he replied.

"These are all termite hills. Different from the towers we will see in Tsavo. The Topi are territorial and this was their way of claiming ground."

How unusual these antelope were! Perched on their mounds, they stood regal and still, almost posing for me while I took a few photos. Their dark bay coats, high sloping shoulders, and their distinctive blue-black abdominal stripe shone in the sun. Turning our Rover around, Darsi continued in a loop. How Darsi and the other drivers navigated the plains of Kenya, I'll never know. It was part of the adventure. My focus was always to enjoy the ride and keep my eyes open.

Back out in the open, Darsi took us off any paths and began to explore in earnest. Soon, trotting out into view from behind some scrubby bushes were two of the remaining five Black rhino males! Two bulls, each with a full set of horns, stopped and stared at us. Lucas turned off the engine. Dr. Erickson and I leaned forward and strained to see every detail. He whispered, "If we stay still, they won't charge."

Black rhinos are notoriously more vicious than white rhinos and are more likely to charge. Being nearly blind, they could mistake a Land Rover for a large animal. Suddenly, one trotted closer, making threatening noises, huffing and grunting. I looked at Lucas to see his reaction.

"If dey get any closa, I will have to back outta here," he whispered calmly. I, for one, was happy to hear that.

We watched nervously as these two 3,000 pound bulls milled around and sized us up. *Would they charge, like that elephant, except worse? If charged, would we be able to back up quickly enough?* Doubtful. My heart started to pound. I suppose this is what real danger feels like— ominous, yet exhilarating. I prayed that our driver had a keen intuition about these things, because these two meant business!

All eyes and ears were on them as they continued to stare at us and make noises. And just as I felt we were beginning to push the envelope, the driver backed up slowly and pulled away. We left our two rhino friends alone. *Had we dodged a bullet?* I thought so, but this great continent of Africa wasn't finished with us yet.

"Wow, that was close," I said out loud.

"It could have been much closer," Darsi quipped. "Nothing like a little rush of excitement, right?" Patrick just shook his head.

Now, I thought, I can take a breath and relax for the remainder of the ride. But that idea was short-lived. Driving through a grove of five-foot acacia bushes, we ran right into a gigantic herd of African Cape buffalo. Lucas quickly slowed to a stop.

"OK, now the hair on the back of your neck can go up," Darsi said in a whisper, as he looked over his shoulder at us.

The buffalo seemed intertwined with the bushes, and as they came out, we could really get a sense of their numbers. Surrounded on all sides, we were in the middle of a sea of black bodies which kept inching closer. Much bigger than domestic cattle, as large as the biggest American Bison, the sheer body mass of these animals was impressive. The horns on their heads spread at least three feet across and they all were staring at us intently.

"How many here?" Dr. Erickson asked.

"I tink probably several hundred. What djou tink, Mr. Darsi?

"I'd say that is a good estimate," Darsi said, looking around. For my benefit he added, "And if they choose to charge as a group, even a small group, we're done."

"That doesn't happen often," added Dr. Erickson quickly. "A lone buffalo is far more dangerous."

The buffalo were milling around and sniffing the air for our scent. Lucas backed us out slowly, and luckily, they accommodated. That was as about as close as I would want to come to these giant bovines.

"I think we are finished here," Darsi said. "Let's turn back, shall we?"

When we arrived, the smells of cooking were enticing. The fire was blazing and the woody smell of smoke hung in the air. We would eat early, Dr. Erickson said, so we could squeeze in an evening game run after dinner. Tonight we would have just spaghetti, in the interest of time. Somehow, these cooks turned even spaghetti into something exotic and new.

Back out in the park, we spent about an hour searching for wildlife. The most memorable we found was a pride of lions resting before the hunt. The females were perched on some mounds of dirt, facing the sun, while the males hung in the background. The glow at this time of day was just enchanting. The setting sun backlit the waterbuck and wildebeest standing in the distance, turning them into silhouettes bathed in a warm halo of light.

"We don't have much time. Look at the light." Dr. Erickson pointed to the horizon. The light was changing quickly. "We need to start back. On the equator, the sun's zenith turns quickly to its nadir."

With our eyes on the horizon, we witnessed the sun's fiery face as it was transforming the sky. The Mara's broad plains provided an excellent view as the blazing, bright, scarlet sun starting to sink. The clouds were turning a shade of eggplant with golden edges. The air was alive with a warm, refracted light. The giant molten mass crashed beyond the edge of the earth at an astounding speed. Even after dipping below the horizon line, at the earth's equatorial bulge, the last remnants of the sun are still visible. It briefly hung there, and then melted out of sight, swallowed by the savannah. Every night it would be the same. There is no twilight at zero degrees latitude. Twelve hours of day became twelve hours of night almost in an instant.

I don't think it was Dr. Erickson's intent to be caught driving as the sun was setting. Soon it would be completely dark. Nonetheless, here we were, the sky turning darker shades and finally, indigo night. Looking up, an immense star-scape was opening up overhead. As if to magnify the savannah, the great wilderness was now above us. The heavens stretched out in all directions, arcing to the ground, unfurling a masterwork of constellations which seemed limitless. The Milky Way was sharply distinct, the stars like white fire, twinkling and blinking.

I didn't know that the phenomenon known as the Celestial Equator even existed, when the skies from the northern and southern hemispheres are visible simultaneously. Then, like silent fireworks, Africa began showing me her spectacular canopy at night. There began a slow cascade of falling stars. Alive and full of movement, it felt like a thousand wishes could come true.

No one was ready to go back to camp; none of us could take our eyes off the night sky. Dr. Erickson assured us we would be able to see these meteor showers every night, if it was clear. Once we got back, we sat by the fire and listened to the sounds of the night, which were all around us. If we were still, we could tune into the crackle of the fire, the whirr of the cicadas and crickets, the forlorn call of a hyena in the distance, all of which vibrated under one ceiling. The fire always brought us together in a way that felt real, and tonight was no different.

"I think you all are doing remarkable well, considering," Darsi said.

"Considering what?" Tim inquired.

"Considering that this is no Muthaiga Club out here." Darsi laughed with his arms out wide.

"Ma– what club?" Tim said.

"*Muthaiga* Club, son. A posh club started for the Continentals. It opened up New Year's Eve, 1913, in Nairobi."

"Ahhh, I see." Tim answered.

"Is that where your parents went to socialize, Dar?" Dr. Erickson asked.

"Oh, eventually, yes. I am a member still. Anyway, you guys are a good group. I haven't heard any complaining, either. This isn't the easiest thing, being out here for so long. Right, Howard?"

"No, it's not. But I guess you have to be willing. And so far everyone's been great. Either you love it or you hate it, I've found."

I listened to the conversation with great curiosity. To me, it became interesting when there was family history involved. I saw Ekevu waiting in the background. Clearly, he had heard this story before. Suddenly, he walked over and sat on the ground in front of the fire with us. He looked at all of us in the circle before he began.

"Did djou know, we have a legend on dis continent dat says our flesh comes from dis earth?" Everyone shook their heads. Darsi just smiled. "And de animals come from dis earth and so does de wind and de fire!" We all nodded, listening intently. "And when de fire lives here," he put his closed fist on his heart, "there is no darkness, no fear. And when we die, our bodies go back to dis earth, but de fire lives on." Entranced, I stared into the fire thoughtfully, letting his words resound in the cool night air.

"Well said, Ekevu," Darsi declared.

"*Asante*," he answered with a nod.

That was Darsi's cue to keep us focused. "OK, guys, time to turn in. We have another full day tomorrow. Don't forget to check under your tents for scorpions before you get in them!"

I smiled to myself. *That is all we needed was a scorpion's bite out here in the back of beyond.*

As I walked by Ekevu I said, "That was beautiful." Ekevu smiled and nodded.

"*Kwa heri*, Miss Hetha."

Once again we were all tired from being in the sun all day, and the many sounds of roaming creatures at night never seemed to keep any of us up, least of all me. Tonight would be no different, scorpions or not.

CHAPTER SEVEN
Mpaji ~ The Giver

"To be yourself in a world that is constantly trying to make you something else is the greatest accomplishment."
~ Ralph Waldo Emerson ~

Even before dawn, the song birds were singing loudly, but it was the light that slowly cut through cool air and the smell of chai that gently awakened me. I faced another morning with just cold water to splash on my face, which would never replace a shower. And there was nothing I could do about my hair. Surely it had taken on a serious look of disarray. Thankfully, with no mirror, I could almost forget how I looked.

From our breakfast table, we had a sublime view across the savannah. A mist hung close to the ground. Slowly, the warm glow of the dawn permeated the dew

and diffused the chill, and the transformation began
again to another sun-filled day. Now that we were in
the heart of the trip, we were exposed to full equatorial
sun all day, every day. Dr. Erickson made it a point this
morning to expand on some basic precautions when in
the Kenyan wilderness.

"Here is the thing. You need to drink a lot of
water in the morning, at least three glasses, and that
should keep dehydration at bay, at least 'til lunch. And
don't touch or stand in any pools of still or stagnant
water, or even rivers, like the Talek. The waters here are
filled with bacteria and parasites that could harm you,
or worse." In his zoology class back at Towson, I had
been studying many of these threats, but it sounded like
there were more. I was curious.

"I thought we were pretty safe. What kind of
parasites are we talking about?"

"Well, for starters, schistosomiasis. It burrows
through the skin – most likely the bottoms of your feet –
and makes its way to your liver and lays eggs. It may
not kill you, but you really don't want that one. Carbon
tablets may be necessary in case we run out of fresh
water and need to drink water that is questionable."
Slightly surprised, I drank the water in front of me and
sincerely hoped that drinking bad water was just a
distant possibility.

After breakfast, I walked to the edge of the Talek
again. She was still running slow and steady. She was

brown with sediment, and it struck me how limited the water supply was for the wildlife as well. At least within several miles, the Talek was the main artery out here. I thought about that as I walked back to the campfire. Within minutes, a small troop of Olive baboons wandered into camp and walked by me, not fifty feet away! I went to get my camera and when I got back, one of the huge males sat down across the campfire from me. Now less than twenty-five feet away, I remained as still as possible and tried not to look directly in his eyes so he wouldn't feel threatened. At two hundred and fifty pounds, he was still a dangerous creature, and if he made a sudden move towards me, I couldn't run fast enough to save myself. So there we sat, enjoying each other's company. The photo later revealed just how near I was—you can see my reflection in his eyes.

Lost in the moment, I almost didn't hear the motors of the Land Rovers starting up. Running over, I jumped in the nearest one, which happened to be driven by Lucas. I squeezed in between Patrick and Tim.

Slightly out of breath, I looked at them and said, "Were you guys going to come and get me?"

"Oh, of course, I would have told them to wait," Patrick said.

"Really?" I said smiling.

"Yeah!" Tim replied sincerely.

I wasn't convinced, but it didn't matter. We were like sardines today, pressed thigh to thigh, which seemed to please both of them. Today, neither Darsi nor Dr. Erickson was with us. It felt like we had lost our leaders and chaperons.

The ride was a bit rough. *Does he know where he is going?* The Land Rover was bouncing and rocking all over the place today. Patrick didn't seem to mind that my body was leaning against his for support, and I didn't either. Tim wasn't blind to this fact and glanced at us once in a while.

When we finally got onto a path beaten down by the grazers, the ride smoothed out, Patrick looked into my eyes and said, "Having fun yet?"

I grinned, "Oh, sure." He smiled back. He was still handsome, even after weeks of being exposed to the elements and with no real shower. I could only imagine how I looked! Permanent dust on my clothes and in my hair, but it didn't seem to repel Patrick. Or Tim, for that matter. I supposed this was a good litmus test for our friendship.

"Hey, look there!" Lucas exclaimed. We turned our heads quickly to see four ostriches walking along nearby. Lucas pulled the Rover up as close as he could.

I can tell you that nine-foot birds look huge in the flesh! Remarkable in their height, but also in their speed, they took off running, gliding gracefully across the savannah. In our Rovers, we picked up our speed and paced them. We opened up the roof and stood up to get a better view. Our cheeks were red, both from the wind in our faces and the exhilaration of the chase, and the ostriches seemed to be having just as much fun as we were! Finally, Lucas let them go ahead and we peeled off to resume our tour.

Sitting back down, I let the brilliant sun that streamed through the open roof rest on my hair and face. What a stellar day! Looking up and leaning back, I let the rays go deep behind my eyes into my brain. The wonderful warmth was a double edged sword, according to Darsi. At this altitude, the sun was closer, and being on the equator meant the intensity was much greater. Yet the cool nights drew you to its energy during the day.

Tim and Patrick were still standing up, but Patrick must have been watching me.

"Is this what you expected from this trip?"

Jolted out of my reverie, I slowly opened one eye and looked at him.

"No, not entirely," I replied. "How about you?"

He sat back down next to me and thought for a long moment as he stared at the passing scenery. "You know, I...I knew it would be rustic but, Africa is just, well, I don't know... unbelievable."

Opening both eyes, I said, "I feel the same way." He turned to look at me, measuring my expression. I smiled. Meanwhile, Tim hopped over the back seat into the front and was talking with Lucas.

"We are looking for de lion," Lucas announced, "and de cheetah; *duma*. Dey like de shade here." Lucas had taken us off the flat onto a slope filled with tall grasses and low-growing acacia bushes. None had seen a cheetah or a leopard yet. Leopards, in particular, are secretive and like resting in trees until they need to hunt. *Maybe this would be our day?*

Sure enough, the bright hillside produced what Lucas was looking for—a pride of lions resting in the shade. They were entangled in the shadows of a several thorny bushes, making them hard to see. The big male stretched and yawned while his harem sprawled around him. I could see how this was a perfect place for them to play during the heat of the day and a wonderful place to rest before the hunt at nightfall. On this July day, they seemed content. We observed them for quite a while.

"What would happen," I asked Lucas, "if I got out and sat closer?"

"Oh, djou don't want to do dat, Miss! At first, it would be fine, but if djou turned to walk away, she might tink djou are a meal and she would charge. Djou never, ever turn your back on de lion!"

"Oh, dear. I didn't know that!"

"Now, why would you want to do that?" Tim scowled from the front seat.

Patrick shot him a look. "She is just trying to get close in for her art!"

"That wouldn't be very smart." Tim rolled his eyes.

"So, guys," Lucas broke in, "we need to move along or we are going to be late for our next stop." Lucas backed off the hillside.

"Late?" I questioned. "For what?"

"Oh, for de balloon ride dis afternoon. We have to get back to camp. Lunch is waiting, my friends."

Then I remembered. I had been offered this option at the beginning, but had had to forego the extra expense. Patrick wasn't going either.

"Are you going, Tim?" I inquired.

"Oh, yeah! I wouldn't miss this!"

Even though I was going to have to pass on this opportunity to see the Mara from the air, I wasn't about to miss the take-off! Ekevu greeted us and served lunch so we could be on our way. Everyone was excited to see this balloon!

Darsi had already gone out to meet the pilot, so Lucas and Ekevu took us out there to meet them. Luckily, the balloon was impossible to miss, and quite the sight out on the savannah. We found it laid out on the grass, basket on its side. It was already inflated about half way. I watched with mixed emotions as the huge nylon skin was filled with hot air from two propane burners. The roar of the burners was intense!

When it was nearly full and the balloon was about to right itself, the passengers got in, like books on a shelf. Tim got in last. The lines were set free and the balloon slowly rose from the ground. Soon, it caught a breeze and was lifted into the afternoon sky.

We all watched as the hot breath of the flames gave life to the giant balloon. Darsi had appointed Lucas as the driver for the chase crew. "Go, man. Follow them! Who wants to go with Lucas? *Hurry.*"

The wind swept the bright balloon over the plains, and Lucas followed as best he could. How marvelous it must be up there! As they drifted onto the horizon and slowly out of sight, I could still see a tiny bright spot of fire and hear the burners roar. Ekevu came over and put his hand on my shoulder. He always seemed to know what I was thinking.

"Miss Hetha, why don't you come with me? De Mara, she has other gifts to see." I turned back to get into his Rover, with Patrick close behind me.

"I hope they know how to land that thing." Darsi said, in his cavalier manner, sliding into passenger the seat. "Let's see if they make it back before dusk, eh bro?" Ekevu nodded.

Darsi was chatting in Swahili with Ekevu almost the whole way back to camp. Patrick and I were lost in thought when suddenly Ekevu put his hand up and said, "Quiet everyone. Look!" He stopped the Rover and turned off the engine.

We had stumbled upon a primeval ritual—a hunt in progress. Two female lions had targeted a wildebeest and were in the process of chasing it down, exhausting it. This was an unusual time of day for a hunt, so it was a stroke of luck that we caught it.

Clearly the wildebeest was already exhausted and the lionesses had already injured it. We watched in horror, as well as fascination, as one lioness came from behind and jumped on the back of the prey, digging her claws into its rear flank and biting right through the spinal cord, just above the tail. While that lioness clung, relentlessly to the spine, the other lioness wrapped her massive jaws around the windpipe of the unlucky wildebeest as it fell to its knees. Both females hung on until the wildebeest fell onto its side. Then, as if that wasn't enough, the lioness on top let go and tore open the abdominal cavity. Life was draining away as the entrails fell out. Shockingly, the wildebeest was still fighting for breath, grasping at life. It took several more minutes for the doomed beast to die. When the two lions looked up, sure of their kill, their mouths and chests were covered in blood.

Today I realized that the scales of justice don't apply; natural laws were the ultimate judge and jury. Life flirted with death often in Africa, and this phenomenon would be played out over and over again. It seemed savage on the surface, yet this was Nature at

her best- *inhuman*. Strangely beautiful, today I saw
Nature dress for the dance; she was in full regalia.

Even Ekevu and Darsi seemed a bit stunned as
we restarted the engine. Patrick and I just looked at
each other, then went back to gazing out the window. I,
for one, welcomed getting back to camp. It was
somewhat empty with so many of us in the balloon, and
it was affording me some time to unplug before they
returned and we ate dinner.

But there was a distinct charge in the air. Maybe
it was from the hunt or the missed balloon ride.
Whatever the case, Patrick felt it too. He asked me to
walk with him. Not far, just to a small acacia tree at the
edge of camps. The acacia's trunk was worn and
smooth, almost without bark, as if animals had been
rubbing up against it. Standing in the shade, I leaned
my back up against the tree trunk facing him. In that
brief second, without hesitation, he came over and
placed his hands on either side of me on the tree. His
toned body moved in and pressed me to the tree. I felt
his weight, his fullness and his anticipation. Then—the
kiss. Surprised, but in the moment, I went with it. It felt
daring and raw, out there in the open. His clothes
smelled of Africa; his skin, like sweat and pheromones.
It was an intoxicating blend. Wishing we were alone, I
felt the passion flowing. But we were within sight of
camp. Suddenly, we both became conscious of that fact.
Patrick took a step back and the thrilling encounter

came to an end almost as quickly as it had started. Giving each other a final glance, we walked back in silence.

I went back to my tent. I didn't know what to think, at first. *Was it the atmosphere, or did he really like me? Was this a one-off, or would it progress?* I fell asleep trying to figure it all out.

The sound of excited voices brought me back from my nap. Tim and the ballooners had arrived and they were bubbling over with stories from above the plains. Tim couldn't say enough. The conversation about the balloon ride carried us through dinner, to the campfire, and deep into the night. Even so, I decided to turn in a bit early, before nine.

As I lay there, the noises of camp started to wind down. People would be in their tents soon, lulled to sleep by the equator's song of insects, birds, and the distant roar of lions. I thought about how at dinner, Patrick had cast his glances my way. He always smiled, but then would always look down. Drifting off to sleep, I wondered what tomorrow would bring… and if anything had really changed for me and Patrick.

"Who's ready for a swim in a pool?' Darsi asked after breakfast the next morning. We never wanted for fresh experiences, but a pool? Out here?

"Really?" everyone said eagerly and in unison. None of us had seen clean water for two weeks, much less a pool.

"Bloody well right!" Darsi said in his casual way, winking. "We're going to make a stop at the Mara Serena lodge. They have a pool and I know they won't mind if we take a dip to wash the road dirt off! Any takers?"

If anyone stayed behind, I don't recall. Bathing suits in hand, we climbed into the Rovers. Cooling off in a pool and washing off some dust was going to be a taste of heaven!

"Yeah, I needed to get supplies for our next leg," Darsi explained. "The pool is just an added benefit, but you guys will like the Serena. It is a luxury hotel, by Kenyan standards, and the lodge sits on top of a hillside overlooking the Mara Triangle, where the Mara River meets the Talek. Ekevu, will you drive? We're going to have to cross both to get there"

"Of course, sir."

"Do we have enough petrol?"

"I believe so, but djou are going to have to get these vehicles serviced soon," Ekevu urged. Darsi agreed.

"We don't want to get stuck out there, particularly out near the triangle." Darsi mused.

"What is it about the triangle," I asked.

"It's sort of like The Bermuda Triangle, accept more predictable. It is the preferred location for poachers to set up permanent camps because it's close to the Tanzania border. They can get rhino horns and meat out of the country efficiently. If someone innocently stumbled into their territory, they might want us, well, *gone*."

Oh my, was there never a safe zone?

In the meantime, Patrick slid into the Rover beside me. Again, I felt his heat. Somehow, out here, emotions became unleashed more easily. We were tuned in more, could feel the shift in energy. Then, as if drawn to the new paradigm between me and Patrick, Tim came to the other side of the Rover, opened the door and said, "Is it OK if I sit here?"

"Sure," I said.

"Are djou ready back there?" Ekevu asked.

"Yes!"

"How are you?" I asked Tim casually.

"I'm fine," he said in a breezy tone. "I've been fine. You?"

"Oh, you know, I'm doin' alright, I guess, for Africa!" He smiled broadly, and I couldn't help but feel his masculine energy, too.

Crossing the Talek was tame compared to the tumultuous Mara, which we almost didn't get across. The brown waters ran fast. Hippos congregated in a pool upstream and crocodiles lurked beneath the surface. Even though we crossed where the water was low, the Rover got stuck in the middle. We all got out and watched as Dr. Erickson came to help Darsi, Ekevu, and all the drivers decide what to do.

Feeling a bit uneasy, I tip-toed to the other bank, moving quickly across rocks that stuck out from the water. In the meantime, hippos surfaced, twitching their ears, breathing, and submerging once again. Thankfully, it wasn't long before the Rover was freed from the grip of the Mara and we were on our way once again. There was a collective sigh of relief.

Soon, we were out on the plains again, making the slight climb towards the Mara Serena Lodge. First there was a rustic sign with an arrow pointing the way. Then, on top of a simple stacked stone marker, a sign said: "4 miles to Serena Lodge." As we turned up a dirt driveway, another sign said: "SLOW DOWN, Bumps Ahead." The paved, well-appointed entrance looked to us like something out of a fairy tale. The sign as you entered the path to the door read:

1°24'09 seconds south of the equator,
35°01'34 seconds east of Greenwich (GMT)
Altitude: 5,321 feet above sea level.

We followed Darsi into the main lobby. He was greeted with open arms, like a long lost friend, as he was wherever he went. The hotel staff greeted us graciously as well, and was more than accommodating when it came to their pool. The layout of the Serena was fashioned after a Maasai village. Each room was a cement building that resembled a single hut. They cascaded down the hillside, flanking the main hotel to provide the most spectacular view of the triangle. The pool was built near the high point of the hill, and from there, we could see all the way to Tanzania, eight miles to the south, and 180° around us.

The Mara Serena was affording us an opportunity to see Kenya from a new angle. We languished unabashedly in the cool water of the pool, savoring our first chance to pause and take in Africa from a position of comfort. For the first time in weeks, we were dust-free, care-free, and close to being clean.

This view from the pool reminded me of our terrace back home. Even though my father had a full-time job, he had managed to design and build a raised fieldstone terrace. He diligently laid one stone at a time and mixed mortar in a wheelbarrow for months. It wasn't nearly as high as this view, but it gave us a spectacular southwest perspective of our valley, including the best sunsets you could imagine!

In the meantime, Darsi was acquiring the supplies we needed for the next phase of our safari. We found him in the lobby, talking to a man behind the front desk. Then another man, who looked like the manager, came into the lobby. They continued their negotiations, and before long, a procession of hotel staff began carrying crates and boxes to our vehicles. As we waited, just listening to my surroundings, I found I was also listening to some of an overheard conversation.

President Moi's name was used several times and it reminded me. I looked around for Moi's photograph, and, sure enough, here he was again, hanging over a doorway.

"...and he thinks he can do that? What else is going on? How does – did – Moi... What does that mean?" Darsi's voice drifted in and out.

His tone was serious when he turned back to us, "Go get everyone together. Find Howard. Where are they all?"

"I am not sure, but I'll go and see," I said quickly.Just as the words left my mouth, Dr. Erickson and the others emerged from a side entrance and Darsi waved them over.

"There has been a small change of plans. I won't be going with you on the next leg of this journey. For the next five days, you will be either climbing Mt. Kenya or going with Howard into the deserts of Samburu on a camel trek."

We all looked at Dr. Erickson and back to Darsi. Nobody had told us about this!

"Do any of you have warm jackets?" A few, including Tim and Patrick, raised their hands. I shook my head, still stunned that he would expect anyone to be prepared for a summit like Mt. Kenya.

I think Darsi sensed my amazement and said, "No, it's OK, you will go with the camels." Before he could say anything else, Dr. Erickson pulled him aside.

He was very animated as he talked to Darsi and I imagined he was speaking for all of us.

When they came back, Darsi continued. "So, we will need to make a decision by the end of today, and then I'll be off!" He made it all sound so simple. "For now, though, you guys need to go wait for me in the Rovers. I need to make a few phone calls. I will be there shortly."

In the parking area, Dr. Erickson helped us digest what was about to happen. "I am not sure what you guys feel prepared for. I've climbed Mt. Kenya many times. It is rigorous, but not impossible, even with no training or equipment."

"I'll do it," said Tim.

"Me too," added Patrick.

Mine was an easy decision. Without any protective gear for high altitudes and freezing temperatures, it was to be Samburu for me. When Darsi finally came back, he looked pensive and was quiet. Before he got in a vehicle, he checked to make sure we had all the supplies he had ordered and that everything was secured.

"Everything OK?" I asked him.

"Yah, I think so," he replied, half-heartedly. I wasn't convinced, but he smiled and we began to drive down the scenic hill, away from the Serena and reminders of home. The sun was getting low in the sky and the herds of wildebeest we drove through seemed to be thicker than ever. Crossing the Mara and the Talek was pleasantly uneventful this time.

Around the fire that night, we spoke of choices that had to be made. Would it be *moto* or *barafu*? Fire or ice? Who was going where and were we prepared for any of it? It was clear that whichever journey we chose, it would be our most challenging adventure so far. And we talked about our time out on the plains of the Mara, especially being on the beautiful Talek River and crossing the mighty Mara. We spoke of all the wondrous things we had seen, the things we would take with us forever.

By dawn the whole camp had a feel of heightened excitement. As we were loading our gear onto the truck, Ekevu came over to me. Standing there, leaning on the Rover and facing the bright golden light of early morning, he looked particularly regal.

He began, "Miss, Hetha, I don't know when I will see djou again, so I wanted to tell djou someting before djou left today..."

"You won't be back when we return?" I asked with concern.

"I ...don't know," he said slowly. "I am going back to Nairobi with Mr. Darsi. A slight change of plans, djou see."

"But, I thought you would be—."

He shook his head slightly and put his hand up. "I am going to drive one of the Rovers back, and Darsi is going to take you to Rumuruti and drop you off."

"OK," I said tentatively.

"Just rememba, life is like dis riva. She is de Giver, *Mpaji*. Find a way to flow with de riva, Miss Hetha."

"Alright, I will." I promised. Not even hearing his words, his tone sounded remarkably like a final farewell.

"But, aren't you—"

He smiled broadly. "*Kwa heri*, for now. Don't worry, dis is not de end."

It didn't feel that way, and I fought the urge to reach out and stop his handsome frame even as he turned and walked over to the supply truck. He looked back at me once, then got in and closed the door. Darsi waved to us to follow his vehicle, and before I knew it, we were off. Still confused, a distinct sadness was creeping into my chest. Without Darsi and Ekevu, it felt like we had lost our compass and our leader, all at once.

I would miss the Mara, too. Being in her midst for five days had been a sincere privilege. She was a bright spot in the tapestry of Africa which left us unconstrained by a schedule. I found myself being caught in the present moment more and more, a most delicious trap, where time can no longer chase you.

As we left, we saw the immeasurable herds of
wildebeests and zebras congregating, preparing to leave the
Mara for those greener grasses of the Serengeti. Instinctively
drawn south, knowing that Tanzania held the key to
survival, the herds kept moving. Like them, our convoy left
The Mara behind.

I would not hear the herds struggling to cross the
steep sides of the great Mara River, or hear them marching
and pushing each other through deep waters where
crocodiles waited. But what my heart did hear made it leap!
I heard the reverberations of the Great Migration, echoing
in all directions. An ageless rhythm, tuned to a sound
greater than us, was calling as they crossed one of the
widest plains on earth to sustain life. I imagined for them it
was like going home. Something I was thinking about, more
and more.

CHAPTER EIGHT
Samburu ~ The Northern Frontier

*"Do not go where the path may lead; go instead where there is
no path and leave a trail."*
~ Ralph Waldo Emerson ~

Darsi had done his best to prepare us for the
Northern Frontier. Just before we began before our
camel trek across the Laikipia Plateau, he had handed
me a small plastic bag.

"Here, take these, Heather. They're dried lemon
peels."

"Thanks. What are these for?" I asked.
"Oh, just suck on them when you get thirsty or run out
of water." I took them, still absorbing what he was
saying.

"You are going to be relying on 'bush-craft' to
survive. Remember to pay attention to your gut. Stay

alert, listen for movement in the bush, and freeze in your tracks, if necessary. I've given Howard some carbon tablets too, which, in theory, will make bad water drinkable." Carbon tablets are activated charcoal. A few dropped into brown water were supposed to buffer the body from harmful bacteria, heavy metals, and general waste. But they give the water a terrible taste, as I would discover.

So now, two days later, walking more than twenty miles a day, I understood what Darsi had been talking about. All I could do was surrender to the path that unfolded before me. *How many hours had I been out here?* It was hard to know. *Was I delirious? Or was the heat just beginning to distort time?* Events were beginning to blur, thinking was difficult. My last images of the sunny plains of the Mara were now juxtaposed with a savagely remote territory that would eventually be described to me as "God forsaken." Ironically, I found myself wishing for the "comforts" of camp life.

The scrublands of northern Kenya seemed intent upon living up to their reputation. Samburu was a hostile wasteland, clothed in orange dust, and covered in sharp volcanic rock, and bushes with three-inch thorns. I carefully threaded my way through them. If scratched, the scent of fresh blood would travel quickly on the breeze and might attract predators. So I pressed carefully on, putting one weary foot in front of another, leaving only a trail of dust.

The lemon peels worked for a day or two, but now, with water being rationed, they were losing their effect. My heart was progressively beating faster and faster. With dehydration a real threat and no shade in sight, we all wished for dusk. Only then could we escape the equatorial sun and get some rest. However, dusk brought out the hunters that lurked in the shadows by day. Every rustle, every movement caught my eye. Exhausted, I decided it was time to ride.

I walked quickly to the lead camel driver and asked for my camel, Saguta. I yanked her lead line to get her attention. *"Chini"*, I said firmly. She stopped and slowly got down on her knees. When her hindquarters followed, I climbed up into the rustic saddle and said, *"Kwenda!"* She got up and resumed her undulating gate, which had been rocking me back and forth for two days now. The creamy ivory bracelet, still on my left wrist, rocked with me.

Looking back, this odyssey had begun with great anticipation just a few days earlier. Together, all of us had just gotten beyond the Talek gate of the Mara, leaving Ekevu and our Unimog truck behind. Then two Rovers followed Darsi, proceeding northwest, and it seemed like a long time before we reached a paved road. Once on the road to Narok, we drove to the Moru Naru road on the west side of Mt. Kenya. There, Darsi had dropped Tim, Patrick, and four others at the road that led to base of Mt. Kenya.

As they pulled over to let them out, a sign said "Meteorological Station." I thought of the monumental task they were facing: climbing a mountain two-thirds the size of Everest. Despite what Dr. Erickson had said, at more than 17,000 feet, Mt. Kenya was equally as technically difficult as Mt. Everest. They would be challenged with altitude and even pulmonary edema, as well as a summit of extreme temperatures, well below freezing. And, with no training and virtually no equipment, they would be taken on a wild ride through layers of habitats so strange, they defied description. When Patrick and Tim peeled off down that road, I regretted not having said a proper good-bye, so I sent a prayer up with them. I thought they would need it more than me.

Our ride from there was smooth at first, paved. But as we crossed the equator and turned left onto Thuthuriki Road, our Land Rover's pace slowed down to a bouncing, rocking gait. As our driver had to negotiate bigger and bigger rocks, even washes and ditches, he was forced down to a crawl. We passed a skeleton of a wrecked vehicle on its side in a ditch, rusty and corroded. It blended with the colors of the earth now, someday to be swallowed by the dust. I can only say, it was a stark reminder.

The landscape had changed; the green grasses were now silvery and dry; trees had become bushes; low mountain ranges rose up in the distance and the earth slowly took on a parched terra cotta color. The wind in my face had turned hot and dry. *Where were we going?*

"Where are these camels? And how much longer until we get there? It seems like a really long ride." I asked Dr. Erickson in the front seat.

"Well, it is about a 200-mile ride to Rumuruti and the Evans place."

"Is that a ranch, or...?"

"Darsi has set us up with a guy named Simon, son of Jasper Evans, who owns a ranch called Ol' Maisor in Rumuruti. Apparently they have camels. We'll trek north into Samburu territory for a few days, then come back." My mind was spinning.

"I know that he also asked Simon for a few more guides, and I am not sure who they are."

He pointed down a lonely road. "See there? This whole area is filled with these huge ranches, all privately owned." Then I remembered.

"Dr. Erickson, my dad knows someone who owns one of these big places, but I have no idea where."

"What's his name?"

"George Small. He's from Maryland, and I wish I had asked my dad more questions now."

"Hmmm, I don't know George," said Dr. Erickson, "but I bet Darsi and Simon do. What is the name of his ranch?

"I think it's *Mpala*. I wish my dad was here. He would love Africa."

"If I remember, I'll ask Darsi when we get back," Dr. Erickson replied.

According to Dr. Erickson, Ol' Maisor was coming soon. I was really getting hungry, so I hoped they had planned lunch for us before launching us out into the wilderness.

"Will the camels be ready to go when we get there?" I asked.

"I don't think so," Dr. Erickson said. "The way Darsi described it is that Simon, or his camel drivers, will have to go find the camels first – they own 30,000 acres – and then catch them."

"You're kidding, right? Will they find them in, what, an hour or so?" I asked hopefully.

"I am as curious as you are as to how this all works. All I know is Jasper Evans, Simon's father, owns this place and had the idea to import camels from India to northern Kenya, instead of raising more goats. Goats are really hard on the land. They tend to over-forage and strip, which is destructive, whereas camels eat less, and give more milk and more meat with less water. And they have the added benefit of being great pack animals for safaris just like this."

Soon, Darsi's Rover turned down a rough driveway, so we followed. At the end was a surprisingly impressive home for being assembled in such a remote territory. Built of a sturdy dark wood, stone, and cream-colored mortar, it was a classically rustic African ranch house with long sloping roofs of red. A front entry porch ran the width of the house. I got out of the Rover to explore and stretch my legs.

Simon came out to greet us. Darsi hopped out and strode over to him, hand out. Again, he was greeted like family.

"*My God*, man! It's good to see you! You look well!" Darsi exclaimed.

"You, too! It's great to see you, Darsi." Simon replied enthusiastically. "Can I get you some refreshments?"

"Oh, not for me, I'm on my way back. But for my friends over here…" Simon looked over at us and waved.

"OK, well, I must shove off, I'm afraid. Just let me say thank you for doing this."

"You are so welcome," Simon said in a deep, clear British accent, as they shook hands again.

Darsi gave us some final instructions and talked logistics with Dr. Erickson, then said good-bye. In the meantime, I couldn't help but notice that Simon Evans was an immensely strong and handsome man. At only twenty-three years old, it was clear that life in the bush had carved him into a muscle-bound survivor. His confidence and demeanor outstripped his years by decades. I immediately knew that he was someone you could believe in; no airs, no pretense, just the real McCoy.

He reminded me of the Lory boys who lived next door to us on Blackrock Road. Henry Lory came from Great Britain at mid-life to begin a new way of living in the United States. He started a second family and bought a farm next to ours to grow cows and harvest milk. All three of his sons were hardy, muscled, and resilient from working the land, eating fresh food, and drinking raw milk.

We introduced ourselves to Simon and he invited us all in for refreshments while he continued to gather supplies. The wide entry hall smelled of ashes and a fire long put out. A frayed oriental rug was soft and quiet under my feet; a far cry from the gravel and dust I had experienced lately. Old English antique furniture lined the walls, as did the skull crowns and horns of African antelope. Even in this rustic abode thousands of miles away, the smells and surroundings felt familiar in a way.

I was handed a tall glass of lemonade, luxurious and elegant. Full of ice, it had been a long time since I had seen anything this cold. He ushered us in deeper, to the back of the hall, where an interior veranda was strategically added for the view. I wasn't expecting what I saw: an overlook of legendary proportions. The house was on a cliff, a thousand feet up, affording us a vantage point that may have encompassed the entire ranch.

Finding The Fire Within

Again, on the horizon, I could barely see lavender hills, a reminder of the immense distance.

Finally, I settled into one of the mahogany wicker chairs, so loved and worn with age they were almost ebony. *Ahhh, to sit in a chair with arms! This feels like home.* While my body rested, my mind was consumed with the powerful scene before me. I sat and stared in disbelief at the view. Miles and miles of uninterrupted wilderness, only the cloud shadows breaking up the distance. Since the Great Rift Valley, there had not been such a thrilling vista!

Waiting for lunch, I tried to envision myself out there. *What was in store for us this time? How far would we go? Where would we camp? Would we have tents?* In the landscape below me, there was a pool of water, probably fed by a small river. *Would that be the last bit of drinkable water we'd see for the next five days?*

Freshly made sandwiches arrived on a tray, courtesy of the Evans' Kenyan domestic help. The thinly shaved roast beef was superb! Later that day, I learned that it was actually bush meat; Thompson's gazelle, to be exact. It was the best red meat I'd ever had! While I savored my sandwich and enjoyed the shade of the veranda, I overheard Dr. Erickson and Simon talking in the in the hallway behind me.

"He's still running about, so I will be taking precautions…" Simon's voice drifted off.

"So, how long has this rogue elephant been out there, causing havoc?" Dr. Erickson asked.

"Oh, I suppose a week now. We haven't been able to get close enough to shoot him yet, so I don't know if he's old or injured. But he'll be lion bait if we don't get him first," Simon added. *A rouge elephant on the loose? It seemed like the stakes just got a little higher.*

After lunch, we had the privilege of freshening up in modern facilities. On my way out, I passed Simon in the front hallway. He was organizing his gear by the front door. This included a massive rifle with a scope. He saw me eying it.

"Do you know what this is?" he said, picking it up.

"I can't say that I do."

"This is a Mauser .375 H & H Magnum. Powerful enough to kill an elephant, if you know what you are doing."

I knew from my limited experience with guns on the farm that shooting to kill an animal of any size is not as easy as it looks, even with a scope. You need a calm presence of mind and all your faculties to be accurate. For this, he had to have the right bullets and know the elephant's anatomy. A misplaced bullet could bounce off its skull or even its tough hide, and turn it into an angry charging elephant.

Meanwhile, the five camel drivers had returned and were out on the veranda. Simon went out to find see if they had located the elusive camels.

"*Je kupata ngamia? Wako wapi?*" Simon asked them.

"*Ndiyo, wao ni nje na kitanda kavu mto dakika thelathini kutoka hapa*" The driver pointed north.

Simon seemed satisfied, and hoisted his gear into an old Land Cruiser parked in front of the house. Next to it, I saw where the drivers had piled up the saddles, food, water tins, and other gear in a heap on the driveway. Then, in the distance, the sun reflected off a cloud of dust. Down the lane came another car, which skidded to a halt in front of the veranda. Two people hopped out.

"Sorry we're late," said a pretty blonde woman in a British accent.

"Yeah, we had engine trouble, small break down. Real pain in the ass!" announced a young, dark haired man, with a slightly different accent.

"It's so good to see you both," Simon said, smiling broadly. Simon gave them a warm hug and handshake. Then he introduced them proudly.

"Everyone, this is Adrienne and Nick. They are friends of mine and will be assisting us on this safari."

We all shook hands. They both seemed genuine and well-spoken, and also quite attractive. Probably only in their mid-twenties, they had not escaped the

African sun entirely. Still, young people were a welcome sight for me, especially since Tim and Patrick were not here.

Never resting long, Simon signaled to his five drivers. *"Mzigo vifaa-sasa!"* Then to us, "Let's go!"

The camel drivers threw all of the equipment, plus our duffle bags, into the Land Cruisers. Drivers were assigned to each vehicle, since we would have to be dropped off. I got into Nick's car, and so did Adrienne. Dr. Erickson went with Simon and the others.

As we tore down the lane and turned north once again, it felt like a whole new world. Being out of the parks meant less wildlife, but it also meant a chance to see species that only lived in the Northern Frontier — the rare Grevy's zebra, Reticulated giraffe, Klipspringers, and more.

Once we got a few miles into Ol' Maisor, we ran into our first snag. The Land Cruiser sputtered and just stopped. Up until now, we had been really lucky with our vehicles, but I remembered what Darsi had said — these vehicles take a brutal pounding and have to be sent back to Nairobi to be worked on every few weeks, and realigned once a month.

The driver hopped out of the cruiser, and so did Nick and Adrienne. At first, I just stayed in the cruiser, but then decided to take a look. As we all peered under the open hood at the oil-stained and dust-covered engine, Nick cursed in Italian under his breath. I smiled. It reminded me of my dad cursing his 1930's Farmall tractor back home. Not unfamiliar with equipment, it didn't seem to me that it was overheated or out of oil, so I prayed for some bush fix. Sure enough, a wire that had rattled loose from rough roads earlier was the culprit, and was fixed in short order. *Thank goodness we weren't marooned!*

Back on track, it wasn't long before we followed Simon off the dirt road into the brush. We drove through challenging territory for about ten minutes before Simon stopped and got out. There were at least a dozen camels grazing, unaware of their impending mission. As soon as the camel drivers were able to capture and harness them, Simon helped his vehicle drivers unload the supplies from the Land Cruisers and sent them back to the ranch house.

The camel drivers approached eight camels, roped them, fitted them with primitive bridles, and got them down to their knees. Next, they got their saddles in place, secured, and packed with supplies. Four camels would be reserved for riding.

I had always heard that camels were hard to deal with, cantankerous and aloof. As I watched the camels being saddled, none of those things seemed true. These dromedaries were docile, acclimated to humans, and seemed well-behaved. In the wild, single hump camels can live up to sixty years, and are perfect for arid environments and the demands of walking long distances. Known as 'Ships of the Dessert', their eloquent design allows them to withstand extreme temperatures and loss of water before they need to refuel. They also have an added benefit of being able to run, for a short while, at forty miles an hour.

The camels were being gathered in the shade of yellow fever acacia trees, where they rested and chewed their cud. Scattered around the camels were pots and pans and a myriad of other stuff. The afternoon sun highlighted the trees and their eerie chartreuse bark. I watched Simon as he walked around and organized a bivouac- type camp site. Then, standing alone over his own gear, I noticed he looked pensive and serious. His short sleeves exposed a pair of muscular biceps that flexed as he loaded his gun.

Meanwhile, Tim and Patrick were right below the equator, at the west face of Mt. Kenya with their guides, at the meteorological station. They would spend the night there and prepare to ascend to the icy pinnacle. It was a three–day ascent, taking the Naro Moru route to Point Lenana. In the process, they would learn, that Kirinyaga, The Mountain of Whiteness, was just as challenging now as it had been for Sir Halford J. MacKinder in 1899. Holding rare equatorial snow like Kilimanjaro, lack of oxygen, altitude sickness, exposure, and exhaustion were their enemies.

So here I was, about to ride camels into the bush for the next several days. It was time to get to know them. I walked up to where they were resting and asked one of the drivers if I could touch them. One caught my attention; they called her Saguta, named after the sand-swept Saguta Valley near Lake Turkana at the northern edges of Kenya. She was sweet and her nose was fuzzy and soft. Her big, kind brown eyes had lashes a mile long. I touched her face and neck, and let her sniff me. I hoped that somehow my years of riding horses would be a plus.

Without a watch, I was oblivious to time passing. I did notice that the day was fading, however. Warm shafts of the sun lit up the camels resting by the acacia grove, and pale grasses shone brightly as purple shadows lengthened. Day resisted the night until it relinquished altogether the last rays of golden light. The camel drivers worked their magic, getting a fire to blaze, and then Adrienne helped them cook a simple dinner.

After dinner, we huddled around the fire, just as we had before, but now we were in our sleeping bags, waiting for a sign to call it a day. Without tents, we could really feel the cold air settle near the ground, and without Ekevu, there was no one to electrify the night with poetic words. I looked up at the canopy of stars and listened for new sounds. The cicadas still created the most noise. No hyenas, no lions, just the occasional rustling of the camels from a stone's throw away. My head on a blanket, I watched the blue wood smoke curl upwards until I must have drifted off.

At first, being out in the open was too stimulating for sleep, as I floated between wakefulness and dreams. Somewhere in the black pit of the early morning, I was suddenly aware that the ground was rumbling, shaking. I opened my tired eyes and lifted my head slightly. It sounded remarkably like the thunder of…hooves? Shattering the stillness, the sound reverberated through the ground and surrounded us like rolling thunder.

What is happening? What is it? Where are they? Confused and groggy, I couldn't see anything! I can still remember the absolute terror and total paralysis that gripped me. I lay motionless in my sleeping bag, hoping it would be over. Only my heart moved, fast and furious, thumping wildly, as if trying to escape from my chest. Slowly, as the sound dissipated, I managed to breathe again, move again. By the time I heard Simon's voice, it had already passed. He added more logs to the remaining coals of our campfire and teased it back to life. Blessed with ignorance, I fell back into dreamland.

CHAPTER NINE

True Bush ~ God was Watching

"If fear is cultivated it will become stronger, if faith is cultivated it will achieve mastery."
~ John Paul Jones ~

I was brought back slowly, eased into reality with the smell of food and tea on the fire. It was then that I remembered.

"What happened last night?"

"It was a stampede. Buffalo," Simon replied. "They must have been spooked. The only reason they went around us was the fire." I could see the tension in his face. "God was watching…"

I didn't know what to say so I sat and quietly sipped my chai. *What would the next five days bring?* There was a new edginess in the air. Africa had drawn

158

me in on blind faith and now, I suppose, it was time to test that faith.

After breakfast, Nick and Adrienne were very active and helpful in getting us packed up and on our way. These two were hardy souls whom you could rely on. When the caravan was packed, we struck out into northern bush country, with Simon in the lead. He was confident as he slung his gun over his shoulder and marched forward. Dr. Erickson followed, then Nick and Adrienne. Behind them, the camels were strung together with lead lines, three at a time, pulled along by one of the drivers. Our water was in twin metal containers on one camel, while our food was on another. Saguta was one of the camels outfitted with a riding saddle, layered in sheep skin.

As soon as I could, I rode Saguta. She was easy to work with and I enjoyed her gait…at first. Up there, I got a new perspective, and while we were still mostly in grasses with the occasional acacia, I thought this might give me some advantage. *Maybe this would be a safer way to go?*

When the grasses turned into more dense bushes, riding became a bit more challenging, so I got off and walked alongside her for a while. Suddenly, a herd of impalas bound past me on my right. My heart jumped, but Saguta didn't flinch. I noticed vultures spinning around a kill in the distance. More rustling came from the bush.

"Don't worry, it's just warthogs," Dr. Erickson assured me. I put my hand on my heart.

"That's good!" I sighed.

After walking for several hours, we stopped for lunch in a clearing next to a solitary patch of trees, almost like an island, calling to us. Leaving the camels to graze in a grassy clearing, we gratefully went into the shade. The leaf litter looked shockingly like the deciduous woodland floor back home, yet it was purely African. Pretty, open spaces let the sun flood in, making it warm and inviting, like soft pine needles. It reminded me that I was without a journal or watercolors; no way to record the beauty. Nature and art invite you in like two old friends; giving you respite for the soul and new breath for the spirit.

For now, fallen timber provided natural benches on which to rest while we ate sandwiches prepared earlier by Adrienne. It was great just to sit down on something solid. Dr. Erickson sat close by, while Simon, aloof and focused, stood on the periphery, eating his sandwich, gun at the ready, keeping his eye on things.

I took this opportunity to ask Dr. Erickson, "Where did Darsi go so suddenly?"

"Well, all I know is that President Daniel Moi has pushed the election forward by fourteen months, to September first this year. It's a one-party state, has been, which means there is too much power in Moi's hands. Kenyans are not exactly happy."

"Hmmm. I didn't realize…"

"Remember, it was only last August that I was caught in the 1982 coup."

"I know."

"The corruption is deep, and the chasm between the poor and the wealthy is broad here, as in most of Africa. I am guessing he went to talk to his friends, make sure there is no more unrest than when he left…and see what the climate is in Nairobi."

I was still digesting all this new information when I got up to look around. I tried to burn every detail into my memory. I saw Simon glance over once in a while.

"Don't wander off," he said in his deep British accent. "We're going to climb this little mountain over here." He pointed behind me.

"I won't." *Little mountain? Hadn't we walked enough?* My shoes were already getting very worn. It was questionable whether they would last the trip at this rate. After we ate, Simon rallied us for the hike, and it wasn't long before the camels were disappearing from sight as we climbed. The mountain didn't look that big from down below, but as we climbed it, I felt the exertion. Grassy paths turned into steeper and steeper paths until they were rocky paths, then just rocks. Even in the dry air, I was starting to perspire, and had to stop once or twice as the air got thinner. The combined altitude of the Laikipia Plateau and this mountain approached 10,000 feet. When I reached the top, the camels were just specks in the clearing.

Back home, I liked to climb tall trees and to the top our barn roof. Once, I had to jump off the top of a full hay wagon that was falling over. Fearless, was the word my mother used for me. I was going to need all of that, and more.

If I had turned around and looked southeast, I might have seen Mt. Kenya. I thought of Tim and Patrick and wondered how they were. We didn't linger long; dusk was coming in a few hours and Simon wanted to cover a certain distance before carving out a campsite, so we made the descent in short order.

In the meantime, Tim and Patrick were at 10,000 feet yesterday. They had driven through the lower forests of Mt. Kenya, comprised of acacias and dense bamboo. By now, they were nearing McKinder's Camp at around 12,500 feet. Muddy buffalo paths would lead them on a rigorous climb through a nearly-vertical bog, where they would sink in and be slowed down. After that, they would have a rare glimpse of a tropical alpine moorland, covered in giant heather. There, plants – lobelias, groundsels, and thistles – would look misplaced and not of this earth. They would pass a mountain lake and see rare birds, like sunbirds, that feed at high altitudes. Rock hyraxes also lived on the mountain. That's a rabbit–sized rodent whose closest relative is the elephant. Below freezing at night, everyone would hunker down and hole up at McKinder's Camp to acclimate to the altitude before striking out towards the summit.

For me, this was the most walking I had ever done and I was starting to feel it. Back in the clearing with the camels, Simon motioned to the drivers, *"Hebu kwenda!"*

Still in mixed brush, grasses, and acacia, we marched on, sticking close to the camels. I passed a partial skeleton, a small antelope, perhaps. Then, the skull of a warthog, unmistakable with its over-sized incisors.

"Watch out for pit vipers," Simon turned around and announced. Then he stopped and went down on one knee. He touched the ground with his fingers, then the grass, then looked at all the foliage at eye level.

"What is it?' I asked.

"Not sure...looking for broken branches, trampled grass, tracks, things like that. So far, no pattern that looks like elephant, but I am sure this rogue is still out here."

We continued through the heat of the day. Nick metered out water here and there, but it wasn't enough. I was looking forward to sitting down again.

In several hours, I was resting by the fire once again. Staring into the flames, I felt a new tiredness creeping in. I was grateful for my hot bush stew and my sleeping bag. Both were warm against the night air. I got into my sleeping bag, listening intently for something out of the ordinary in the night. Just the insects. Exhausted, I fell asleep.

Morning brought an awareness of mild thirst. I made sure I drank the water that was allotted. Never one to linger long in the dawn hours, Simon struck out early while the sun was still young. On foot at first, I soon thought riding Saguta was the answer. But the gait of a camel strains the back and rattles the bones, so I only could do that for a few hours a day.

We went progressively deeper into the arid land of Samburu. There was no question now that we were in desert conditions. The ground got drier, and sprouted less and less grass. It was dense with bushes covered with long thorns – almost white – making them look gray as ghosts. Despite the fact that this was cheetah country and the land of Grevy's zebras, we encountered little wildlife. I was told that farther north, there were Kudu, Gerenuk, and Dik-dik antelopes. So far, it was just their bones.

It was about this time that Simon put his hand up. We halted. He motioned for Dr. Erickson and Nick to come to the head of the line with him. Then he spoke to them in soft tones.

"I want you to start picking up small rocks and throwing them into the brush ahead of us. If anything is out there, I want it to hear us before we hear them."

The eyesight of a lion is five times better than ours, and they can hear you from a mile away. Simon didn't need any surprises. Back about one hundred feet, I listened to the *click-clack, click-clack* of the stones falling through dry branches and hitting the earth. For the rest of the day and into the next, I heard this over and over again. It was an eerie sound, reverberating outward like the ripples on a pond. A hollow sound, foreboding somehow as the stones hit dead branches.

As we got into thicker brush, so did the tension. I found myself listening to the sound of my own footsteps. *Was I quiet enough? Would I attract anything?* The camels' soft, wide, twin toes were perfect for this land and made almost no sound at all. Giant thorns reached out to grab my shirt and my skin. These were nothing like the hedgerows back home, with just their small barbs. I stopped to catch my breath and looked closely at this gigantic pointed undergrowth. I touched the long three inch shaft of one thorn, marveling at its needle-like sharpness. The sunlight caught the jagged pattern of the bush and threw the shadow onto my khaki shorts, and I truly understood camouflage. Shadow and light danced together to fool the eye. I am sure Simon was counting on this to work in our favor, albeit momentarily, if necessary. We needed every advantage.

Onward we went, trekking into territory that had now changed into shades of tan and grey. Rocks sprouted up here and there in the rusty earth, which I navigated with Saguta, walking beside her. The sun was relentless now; thirst and hunger were now always present in the background. I imagined Tim and Patrick felt the same, except they were cold and having a hard time catching their breath.

After a brief lunch, Simon pressed us to move forward. He had a destination in mind. Little did we know we were about to cross one of the wildest, most rigorous and untouched places in Kenya, unfriendly to man and beast alike. Heading north, Simon started to move us through as quickly as possible. Meanwhile, it was more important than ever for Dr. Erickson, Nick, and Simon to resume rattling the underbrush with rocks. I was about fifty yards behind with Saguta, and everyone else was behind me in varying distances. Ahead of me on my right was a stand of elephant grass.

Also known as Napier grass, it's similar in structure to sugar cane, but as tall as an elephant.

Suddenly, Saguta stopped and perked up her ears. I hadn't seen her do that before.

"What is it, girl?" I whispered.

I looked around, then paused and listened. There was a rustling, a whooshing sound. *Where was it coming from?* Saguta was not budging. I could see no one from my group, nor anything in the undergrowth. My heart started to beat wildly.

Then, out of nowhere, *thwack!* A gunshot rang out! I jumped. The bullet's percussion resonated through the bush and through my body. My nerves were on edge as I stopped dead in my tracks. Uncertain of what to do next, I did nothing. *Should I hide?* My blood was pounding in my ears. Then two more shots, a slight pause, then three more. *My God, what would need six shots? Was it Simon? Or someone shooting as us? Poachers?* Not knowing whether to go forward or stay, I remembered Darsi's advice, and I froze. Then, after a few minutes of silence, I pushed past the fear and cautiously moved toward the area of commotion.

I made my way through the brush until I found them. I'll never forget what I saw next. Simon was standing over a massive Cape buffalo carcass which reached up to his waist, oozing blood from its many bullet wounds. The veins in Simon's muscled arms were bulging as he rested his rifle stock on the ground.

With the other hand, he used a handkerchief to wipe the sweat pouring off his brow. Managing to look calm and introspective, he surveyed this immense creature.

The camel drivers talked excitedly; *"Tulipoteza ngamia wetu na maji!"*

Simon pointed and yelled, *"Well, go get it! Nenda kupata-haraka!"* to one of the camel drivers. "What are you waiting for? *Go!"*

"Oh, my God! What happened? Is everyone OK?" I said, trying not to sound panicked.

"What a bloody surprise!" Simon chuckled. "Out of the blue, here comes this bull, wounded, mad as hell. He went through the elephant grass, skimmed by Maggie once, came back around and charged the camel with water, knocked her over. When I shot him, he turned on me! I had to drop him – six shots in all – not fifty feet in front on me. "

"Wow," I gasped. It took several minutes for me to wrap my brain around all this. The buffalo's head was twice as big as a steer's head back home, and the rack was as wide as my outstretched arms.

"The water camel ran off. I sent the drivers to get her back," Simon explained, as he pointed. "I hope they do!"

Just then, Dr. Erickson walked over and announced, "Well, they did find the water camel, but it seems that two drivers just left. I guess they think they're safer walking off into the bush. Going home, I guess."

Simon just shook his head. "Well, I can't worry about that. I have to carve this son of a bitch up right now, before he attracts more than vultures!"

I watched as he got out a huge skinning knife and started to cut through the thick hide. Something about the smell of the blood from the carcass, the sun and the heat – all of it was making me feel queasy. I stumbled over to the nearest yellow fever acacia and plopped down in the shade on my back with my eyes closed.

When I opened them, the crunchy brown grass underneath me reminded me of where I was. Up through the beautiful yellowish-green branches of the acacia, I saw a crystal cobalt sky. How spectacular the colors! Then I noticed them, through the branches. There were no less than a hundred vultures circling above me. The buffalo a few yards away had brought them here, but I wasn't ready to be on the menu, too. I tried to get up, but my head was spinning and I had a cramp in my side, so I surrendered back down to the ground.

Then I heard voices. "Are you OK?"

Tim and Patrick were being asked these very same questions by the guide on Mt. Kenya. They had left MacKinder's Camp at 3A.M. in order to get a jump on the final climb to the summit. Managing altitude

169

sickness on little sleep was challenging. More rigorous than the vertical bog and slippery paths, the last 6,000 feet of Mt. Kenya was treacherous. Her final ascent made breathing nearly impossible, every step hard won. The twin snow- caps, Batian and Nelion, were wind swept and steep. After hours of struggle, they finally reached the summit, exhausted.

In my case, Dr. Erickson and Nick knelt down next to me. They touched my forehead and felt my pulse.

"I just feel really weak and shaky."

"Well, you're probably just dehydrated, and probably some heat exhaustion. We'll get you some water," Dr. Erickson said. Which they did, but it had a carbon tablet in it, so it tasted like I was drinking ashes.

"I know," said Nick, smiling at the face I was making, "it's horrible, but we are not taking any chances."

Simon came over to see what was going on. He was still wiping the blood off his hands and arms with his handkerchief. His shirt was spattered in blood.

"I got the tenderloins out. We'll have them for dinner. How are you, Heather?" Simon kneeled down beside me and touched my forehead.

"Oh, I guess I am fine." I rested on my side on one elbow.

"You are a bit overheated," he said. "When you're ready, I am setting up camp over by that pool."

"Don't stand in it, or touch it," added Dr. Erickson.

"Alright," I said, weakly.

By dinner, after resting and recovering in the shade, I did feel better. I walked over to this pool of water. In truth, the pool was really part of an oasis, complete with palms growing out of the huge rocks that framed the brown water. The rocks were wet with the spring water dripping from the crevices. It was odd to see wet rocks covered in lichen here. For me, it was another painting to remember, for when I got back to my paints.

Over at the bustling campsite, Adrienne had soaked the buffalo meat in a papaya marinade for the last few hours, and had baked a cake using a reflective oven. The fire was ablaze as Simon and Nick turned the spit they had rigged for the main course. The sun had set and a white crescent moon had risen in a clear purple sky behind the oasis, making the men appear almost mystical as I stood, watching them prepare our food. The light from the fire was now the focal point and came alive as the meat juices dripped into flames, spitting and popping. The crackling blaze sent up sparks like flares, lighting up the scene. The meat was delectable and natural-tasting, albeit a bit tough. The fireside talk that night was all about the buffalo charge.

"Considering our options, the buffalo was a blessing all round." said Simon, in a serious tone. "He was definitely wounded. It looked like arrows from the Maasai or Samburu."

"He'd probably been wandering the bush for hours, maybe days," added Nick.

"I think you saved him from a long, agonizing death," Dr. Erickson interjected.

"I agree," Simon nodded.

Dinner over, Simon walked over to his knapsack and took out another shirt. He pulled off the blood spattered one, and in the fading firelight, I could see his sizable chest – bare, well-formed, and so masculine.

After eating as much as I could, I wandered over to the oasis one more time and stood looking at the moon reflected in the still pool. I thought of my fellow travelers on Mt. Kenya. It would have been nice to have a comforting hug – at least – from Patrick. And I missed Ekevu and wondered what he was doing tonight. *Would I ever see him again?* I was sure of one thing. Tomorrow we would head back, and I would get to see Tim and Patrick.

I was happy to take off my shoes and let my blistered feet breath. Lying in my sleeping bag and looking up at the stars, I really was missing home. Right about now, in the heat of the summer, dark and ominous thunderstorms would be rolling across our valley with lots of lightning, which was the entire reason my dad had decided to lower the barn by fifteen feet several years ago and install lightning rods. It was

only a month ago in early June that my sister and I were
in the hay wagons, catching forty-pound hay bales out
of the baler and stacking them in the wagons. Dust and
strands of hay stuck to our sweat-drenched shirts and
in our hair. Then, in the oven-like rafters of our barn,
we threw the bales up out of the wagon and stacked
them thirty feet high, until they touched the rafters.

I remembered one time when my father and I
dug a very long trench from the house to the barn in
rocky Maryland soil, in the heart of August, which
meant that the sweat never stopped dripping off my
nose. I could picture how the lawn and fields looked
right now: an endless sea of grass as it engulfed every
fence post, every tree, and hugged all the buildings—
the barn, the log springhouse, and the smokehouse.
And the cattails, which I was sure were growing
happily without me, would be my job to manage.
Sometimes, there were so many cattails that when I
pulled them up and stacked them, they made a raft so
big I could float my entire body on it! I didn't miss
raking the algae, though. I smiled and drifted off to
sleep.

The soreness in my feet brought me back to
reality at dawn. They weren't much better, but I put my
shoes back on and hobbled over to the dwindling fire.
The camel drivers had made some form of chai. It
wasn't as good as Ekevu's, but I welcomed it
nonetheless. As I sipped it and stared into the hot coals,

I wondered when we would turn back to Ol' Maisor. My plan was to ride Saguta as much as possible now.

Adrienne made us a special breakfast, complete with eggs and strips of buffalo meat. When breakfast was over, they made sure they extinguished the campfire thoroughly because of the dryness. And I knew from the carbon tablets in the water I had drunk the day before that we were running out of water.

I saw Dr. Erickson and Simon conferring with the remaining the camel drivers. Simon loaded up the camels himself today. I walked over, waiting for a break in the conversation.

"How far north are we, Simon?"

"We are getting close to the Chalbi Desert, which is just north of here, near Lake Turkana. We're taking a slight detour, a straighter route back. One of my drivers just told me that some Ethiopian refugees are crossing into Kenya and I want to avoid that for now."

"Ethiopian refugees?"

"Yah, well, that country has been experiencing a drought, which is now looking rather serious. They have cyclical droughts, but this seems to be much worse. They are crossing the Chalbi to look for food and water, and I don't know what I can do for them right now," Simon said in a flat tone.

"That is terrible...awful," I replied.

Dr. Erickson chimed in, "If they can make it to Lake Turkana, at least they could find water."

"That is true, but they might even have to come as far as the Ewaso Nyiro River. OK, no time to waste, let's get going," said Simon.

He turned to his drivers and shouted, *"Tandiko juu!"* We moved off, back into the bush, back through the maze of flora and fauna. My clothes smelled of wood smoke, and the ever-present dust stuck to my skin and had invaded every corner of my life. My bracelet seemed to have grown much whiter in the past three days as the sun turned me browner. My blistered feet were bothering me. By mid-morning, nothing mattered except food, water, and making it through another day.

It wasn't long after that that we got a glimpse of some bedraggled, bone-thin people in the distance. When you see another human in dire need, everything else seems to melt away. *How can so much of the world be so desperately hungry?* It was hard to wrap my tired mind around it, but I carried that image with me for the rest of my journey.

Simon and Nick stayed in the lead and remained cautious for the rest of the walk home. They continued to rattle the bushes and toss rocks into the unknown. Now that our supplies were very low, we couldn't afford any more shocks.

It took another day and a half to get back to the spot Simon had prearranged as our pick-up point, where a couple of Land Cruisers were waiting. The camel drivers dismantled all of the gear from the camel saddles and then threw the saddles into back of one vehicle, and we drove back to the ranch house in another. I took a moment to say goodbye to Saguta, who had turned out to be so easy to like. I would miss climbing into the saddle and riding up and down with her. The camels were set free and the camel drivers literally walked off into the bush again, headed back to wherever home was, disappearing like mist on a sunny morning.

The green lawn at Ol'Maisor looked amazing to me as we pulled up to the house. Darsi, chatting it up with one of his own drivers in the front yard, was a welcome sight! I was thrilled to be back to some semblance of the modern world.

Simon and Darsi immediately engaged in a lively chat, and I realized it was going to be harder to say goodbye to Simon than I had previously thought. *What do you say to a man like that?*

I decided to say goodbye to Adrienne and Nick first.

"Thank you for *everything*. I'll never forget what you guys did out there."

"Oh, you are welcome!" Adrienne said in her sweet British accent.

"Our pleasure," Nick chimed in, in his Italian accent. "No problem at all." He winked as I shook his hand.

Then I went over to where Simon and Darsi were now locked in conversation, no doubt over the recent events on our trek. Hanging on the periphery, the right words were hard to find. Good-byes had become part of my experience here; meeting wonderful and unique people, and then letting them go, probably forever. After Darsi and Simon shared a warm handshake, I stepped in.

"Simon, I can't thank you enough for this trip. It was, well, wonderful...and I'll never forget it."

In his deep and emotionless voice he replied, "You are welcome, Heather. I hope you come back someday. Maybe then you can bring your husband or some thing." He smiled.

"I would love to come back! I'm not sure when." I smiled back.

"Well, whenever it is, it will be a good day." He reached out to shake my hand. His firm grip was sincere and warm.

"*Kwa heri*, Heather."

"*Kwa heri*," I echoed, trying not to tear up. I went back to the Rover and, without ceremony, we were off again. But as we kicked up dust going down the lane, there was a smile in my heart.

Tsavo was calling, a part of Africa that was inhabited by vast elephant herds and red dust that ran like blood in the rain. A park so big, it claimed ten million acres. For a short time, it would claim us too.

CHAPTER TEN

Tsavo ~ The Shared River

"Nearly all men can stand adversity, but if you want to test a man's character, give him power."
~Abraham Lincoln ~

Darsi had his foot to the floorboards as we made our way down the Naro Moru Road to the base of Mt. Kenya to pick up Tim, Patrick, and the others. I was in the front seat and the only passenger for a change, and got the full effect.

"You are not going to believe what is going on in Nairobi with *Moi*..." Darsi began. "He has somehow managed to push his election forward by *14 months* to September this year! Bloody hell! What is he thinking? He's already criticized and disliked by the people ...people are *already* really upset. They are still reeling from last year's coup. And now this? And *trust me,*

179

there is corruption in his administration *and* his party, including turning a blind eye to poaching. In fact, poaching has skyrocketed since the ban on killing elephants in 1973." His British accent got a bit shrill in the excitement.

Lost in thought and tired, I was only listening half-heartedly to his rant up until then. But now he had my attention so I broke in. "Do you mean the Kenyan government *knows* about poaching, or that they are *involved* in it?" I asked.

"Oh, I am sure they not only *know* about it, but are finding a way to *profit* from it! As long as Asia thinks that bush meat and ivory have special powers, the market will persist." Darsi's voice was charged with emotion.

"God, *really*? You're kidding?"

"I wish I wasn't."

"That's unbelievable..."

"Well, *get used to it.* Anytime you have a one party state, especially here in Africa, you can *bet* that all kinds of shit goes down behind the scenes. People get cocky and think they are untouchable." Darsi added pessimistically.

"Makes me glad I am part of a democracy, I guess." I added quietly, not knowing what to say. Darsi threw me a glance that was skeptical at best. I wished we had passengers right then; they would have been entertained. It was hard to believe the stark reality that

Darsi was describing. Ironically, we were about to enter into one of the biggest parks in the world and home to two-thirds of Kenya's elephants. It was a sobering thought.

We skidded on the gravel as we turned into the Meteorological Station. The sun was getting low in the sky and I know Darsi wanted to get into Tsavo West by nightfall. I couldn't help but notice how tired Tim and Patrick looked as they walked towards the rover. I hopped out in anticipation of their greetings.

"My *God*, it is good to be off that mountain!" Tim exclaimed as he hugged me.

"Me too." Patrick chimed in. We locked eyes and then he gave me a big hug! It seemed like they had been gone for weeks, not days.

"So, how was it?" I asked curiously.

"Oh, gosh…you have no idea!" Tim said as he gave Patrick a knowing look.

"*Challenging…*" Patrick commented.

"Yeah. To say the least." Tim said quietly.

"Come on, get in. You can chit- chat on the way!" Darsi called to us. We squeezed in and sped south until we reached Mombasa Road. There, we turned southeast towards Mombasa and Tsavo.

Both Tim and Patrick looked wrung out, and Tim's cough was worse. As they described the altitude sickness and how they shivered every night in their sleeping bags, it was clear they needed a break and some rest. After I shared my experience on the camel trek, I think they were glad they had only the mountain to navigate.

Even though the wear and tear was showing on all of us, now that I was sandwiched between Tim and Patrick in the back seat, the world did seem right once again. As we drew closer to the top entrance of Tsavo and the beginning of the Chyulu Hills, one last piece was missing.

"Where is Ekevu?" I asked Darsi.

"Oh, you'll see him soon. He's driving the Mercedes truck loaded with supplies. Probably already there at the campsite. I told him to get there in time to set up before dark."

"OK, good," I responded. Darsi looked in the rearview mirror and grinned at me. *Oh, it will be good to see Ekevu again, and his smile.* Plus, I was sure he had a few stories waiting for us.

At the Mtita Andei Gate, we slowed down, but only momentarily. The sun was dropping quickly. We had less than an hour before the final rays of light would be gone. Looking ahead, a red dirt road pulled us into a huge wilderness framed with distant mountain ranges. On these dirt roads, which led into vast wild places, we would kick up so much dust over the next three days that we would be stained by laterite, the red component in the soil.

Nevertheless, at this wonderful time of day, Tsavo showed us how lovely she could be. The afternoon light hit the road with long brushstrokes as the red soil gave up its dusty pink highlights, its hues of vermillion and mahogany shadows. The mountains released their hold on the subtle purples and blues in the crevices and valleys. The occasional acacia tree and pointed ridges of the distance were silhouetted by a sky colored in creams, yellows, and soft blues.

Rugged by nature, I could see that Tsavo had a unique and captivating beauty all her own. We were all immersed in the new picture we saw out our rover windows when Darsi announced, "We're almost there, gang!" We all brought our attention back inside.

"I'm starving!" said Tim.

Fortunately, Ekevu had arrived on schedule with the camp staff and had orchestrated a warm meal, ready to be served. I smelled the cooking food in the air as I got out of the vehicle. We all threw our stuff in a pile, and like moths to a flame, flocked over to the campfire where Ekevu was waiting.

"Ekevu!" I exclaimed.

"Hetha! Ahhh...it is so good to see *dyou*!" He extended his hand and I gladly shook it. He looked refreshed and rested with a clean white safari shirt. Only buttoned half way up his chest, you could almost feel the hard muscles of his chest.

"I am so glad to be back, to see you... and everyone." I added.

"Well, the earth does need de rain, right?" His face lit up.

"So true," I said with a grin.

"What djou need? Djou look tired, Memsahib." Ekevu remarked.

"Gosh, Ekevu, I don't know... a real bed, maybe some cow's milk with ice? Coffee? A hot shower perhaps?"

"I cannot give djou *those* tings, I am sorry..." Ekevu smiled.

"Maybe a washing machine, a hair dryer, new shoes? Look at me!" I laughed. "New clothes? What do you think? "

Ekevu laughed, "I see dat dyou *are* a little dusty."

"*A little!*" I exclaimed.

"Well, how about some hot stew, made by me, just tonight?" And let me take your clothes, Miss Hetha, and wash dem?"

"Oh- that would be *wonderful!* Thank you."

I was feeling better already, like I was home. He grabbed my duffle bag for me and escorted me over to a tent. "Here djou are, dis is your tent," Ekevu said, with his arm outstretched.

I threw my duffle bag inside the tent. "I'll be right back."

Inside, I took a deep breath. *God, it will be great to get rid of these clothes.* Quickly, I started to take off my clothes, but then I hesitated. I became highly aware that the only thing separating me from Ekuvu was a single layer of canvas. Proceeding more slowly, I peeled away everything down to my bra and panties. Ekevu waited patiently to take my clothes. When I handed them off through the tent flaps, his hands brushed over mine. His touch was so tender even though his palms were rough from hard work.

Turning to walk away he said, "Don't worry, Miss Hetha, Tsavo will share some of her dust with djou too."

Shortly, I joined everyone around the fire. Everyone was noticeably quiet as they ate, all of us grateful for food that was hot, prepared by someone we knew and with recognizable ingredients. And, were all still recovering from the last four days, no doubt.

"What is wrong with you guys?" Darsi said suddenly. "My brother Hans and I have taken safaris that lasted weeks, from Nairobi to Zimbabwe, to Rwanda and Burundi..."

Ekevu stood up and said, "Why don't I tell dem a story? Maybe de story..."

"...of the legends of Tsavo?" Dr. Erickson added.

"Dat is exactly right! Djes, sir." We all turned expectantly as Ekevu sat back down and looked into the fire gathering his thoughts.

"Well, my brothers and sistas, a long time ago, before de time of motor cars, de British decided to build a railroad. Born in Mombasa, dis iron snake, she winds her way up through Kenya all de way to Lake Victoria. Dis railway was built on de backs of many, many people from India…and many people never came back. But when dey got to de Tsavo Riva and tried to build a bridge across her, dat is when de trouble started…" We all waited, hanging on his words.

"At night, de workers started to disappear…like ghosts into de darkness. Workers were being pulled from their tents while dey slept…*gone*… And no one knew what was happening. Dey built bigger fires and put thorn fences around de camps but *noting* worked. Many men fled and left de railway…and then dey figured it out. There were two mane-less male lions who had been killing and eating de workers. Dey got a taste for human flesh… killing and eating over one hundred men before de lions were shot."

"Whoa…" Tim whispered under his breath.

"Yes. And *dat*, my friends, is how de Man-eaters of Tsavo got their name… "

Dr. Erickson added, "This is the Uganda Railway, really. Somewhere along the way it got the

name *Lunatic Express.* We will be riding that rail in a
few days from Nairobi to Mombasa, so get ready!"

"Thank you, Ekevu, well done," Darsi
remarked. "I think almost 2,500 men lost their lives out
there just building it, right, Ekevu?"

"Dat is right."

"Goodnight everyone. Sleep tight." Darsi said
getting up. "See you at sunrise." He walked into the
darkness.

We nodded and said goodnight and then Ekevu
added, "Don't worry, there are very few lions who ever
get de taste for humans."

"Well, that's good." I said under my breath, and
standing up. Tim and Patrick both looked at me as if
they wanted me to stay. "See you guys. I'm exhausted."
Tim and Patrick stayed and talked to Ekevu well into
the night.

I was really looking forward to sleeping in a tent.
Oh, how your perspective can change. I wrapped myself in
my old quilt and snuggled inside my sleeping bag, letting
dreamland take hold. Even first light and the sounds of
camp didn't wake me up. Clearly, I needed the extra rest
and I know I wasn't alone in that.

CHAPTER ELEVEN
Revelation~ The Savage Red Earth

*"What we call Man's power over Nature turns out to
be a power exercised by some men over other men with nature
as its instrument."*

~ C. S. Lewis ~

With morning, came a fresh day and fresh
clothes, neatly folded and delivered outside my tent. As
I got dressed, I could smell the spices coming from the
hot chai on the fire. We all came to the breakfast table
relatively late. Both Tim and Patrick were rather
subdued. Tim looked particularly tired.

"What day is it?" Tim asked.

I shook my head. "I have no idea. Mid-July?"

"We definitely missed the 4th of July," Patrick
added. Then he asked me, "Do you want some eggs and
bacon? I'll get you some."

"Oh, that would be nice, thanks. And chai, please," I smiled.

"No problem." Patrick looked more rested and the sparkle was back in his dark brown eyes.

When he came back with the food, Darsi walked by and noticed our late start.

"OK, guys, look lively," he said cheerfully. "You are about to get acquainted with this place." We all looked at each other and then took our time eating.

When it was time for us to get up and into the Land Rovers, Tim still seemed tired. I looked at him.

"I think Mt. Kenya got the better of me," he said. I nodded.

All three of us gravitated towards Ekevu, who was waiting patiently by one of the vehicles.

"Ready for Mzima, you three?" asked Ekevu.

"I suppose we are ready as we'll ever be. What is *Mzima*?"

"Mzima means "alive"! It is a spring that comes from underground, all the way from the Chyulu Hills. She is an oasis, djou know, and is de home of many beautiful animals and lots of birds. Djou will see."

We were bumping along Tsavo's western edge, going south, when we started to witness her volcanic beginnings. Her beauty fell from cliffs and rolled across the land, springing up in the form of craters and the skeletons of long lava flows. Around us were

189

misshapen acacia trees against magnificent open land with some of the broadest views in east Africa so far.

Occasionally, we were lucky enough to see a colony of weaver birds on the trees. Dozens of round thatched nests hung from the tips of the branches like Christmas ornaments. In an old dead tree was a Maribou stork, looking rather gothic. We came upon the kill that had brought the stork close to the road. It was being fought over by marabous, hyenas, and vultures. It was odd to see a stork amongst them, but here in Africa, even storks were scavengers.

Driving further south, Ekevu pointed to the right. "Dey are de Chyulu Hills and de end of the Shetani lava flow. She is de longest in de world. De water dat comes to Mzima is born here and takes its time, many decades, to be cleaned by dis lava rock. When it appears, it sparkles!" Ekevu looked at us in the back seat and smiled.

"I can't wait to see it. It'll be good to see some clean water for a change," I remarked.

"And here in front of us is de Nguila Escarpment." It rose up 4,000 feet, seeming to tower over us. Soon the landscape ahead was markedly greener and I could see a patch of trees, just like around the Talek River, gripping the springs. This time, along with figs, there were raffia palms and waterberry trees, which bear fruit that vervet monkeys and birds rely on for food. Living among these trees was wildlife and birdlife that remained disguised in the shadows. But what lay under the water's surface was a whole world unto itself.

"OK, we are here," Ekevu said. "Before djou guys get out, I wanted to tell djou, there is an underground pod built below de water. Djou can see who lives here from there."

Ekevu showed us the concrete steps which led us down into an underground concrete chamber giving us a submerged view of Mzima. Right away we spied the main residents: hippos! Through the pod's glass windows, we saw their world. We watched in awe as hippos floated by as if on tip-toes, almost gravity free. Occasionally they would rise to the surface, snort, and go down again. Fish scooted by, avoiding the hippos, as most creatures would. But also lurking in the waters were Nile crocodiles, one of the most feared of all reptiles.

Back at the surface, I watched a family of Egyptian ducks swim by, enjoying what was turning out to be a stellar day. The air was intensely fresh and the cobalt sky was filled with giant white clouds that were reflected in the water. White egrets stood like marble statues, poised on low branches, waiting for unlucky fish. A little higher up, Malachite kingfishers flashed iridescent feathers like rare jewels in the sun. Cormorants also perched nearby, black feathers disguising them in the shadows. Vervet monkeys watched us and chattered incessantly.

Ekevu and Darsi had probably seen this place a dozen times, so they hung back with the other drivers while I snapped a few photos. I noticed that Patrick looked bored and Tim seemed disengaged altogether. Even though I was tired from walking in Samburu, my intent was to soak up all that I could. Once in a while, Patrick threw me a glance and smiled.

Soon it was time to move on and we hopped back in our Rovers. "So, what else is there to see in Tsavo?" I asked Ekevu.

"Oh, well, let's see. We will see de elephant and de zebra and de giraffe. We might see a leopard or cheetah." I still had not seen either one of those big cats.

"What about antelope and lions?"

"Of course, Miss Hetha. Always de lions." He smiled. "Dey are out there. Tsavo, she is a big place!"

We drove by a particularly scrubby area and to our right was a hillside piled with boulders. Ekevu slowed down and appeared to be looking for something. Then he stopped the Rover.

"Look there!" Ekevu whispered excitedly and pointed to the rocks.

We all leaned towards the windows. At first, we saw nothing. Then a tiny grey-brown creature could be made out against his matching background. It was a Klipspringer, one of the smallest antelopes in the world.

Only twenty inches at the shoulder, his little body and horns looked delicate and refined against the rough lava rocks. His hooves were perfectly designed for jumping over crevices and staying balanced. I quickly took a picture. So as not to scare the little antelope, we pulled away slowly.

"I want to show djou guys someting else," Ekevu said quietly.

"Sounds good," said Tim.

Ekevu came upon what he was looking for in short order.

"What is that?" exclaimed Tim.

"What in the world...?" I asked.

"Dat, my friends, is de work of termites; that's their home. See, around here, termites are our earthworms, dey make sure de earth is aerated and enriched."

"Wow!" we all said in unison. What we were seeing out our windows was a five-foot tall structure that looked like a tower of sand drippings, but instead, it was made from the reddish soil.

"People are just not going to believe the things here," Patrick said.

We all nodded our heads, still looking at these amazing works of natural architecture. And as we drove on, there was more! It may have looked like it was just dirt, but the termites saliva that held it together made it as hard as concrete.

Finding The Fire Within

Our final stop before returning to camp was the Chaimu Crater, in the Chaimu Hills. When we arrived, Darsi and the other Rovers were already there. Dr. Erickson was out wandering with a few of our party, so we hopped out and caught up with him.

"This crater is only two hundred years old; it's a baby in the birth order of eruptions," Dr. Erickson explained. "And, if you notice, the lava that bubbled up created air pockets — caves where fruit bats live, and other creatures."

We walked around the base of the crater looking for these caves, which were overgrown with acacia bushes and other vegetation. Tim, always bold, stuck his head into one.

"Be careful," Dr. Erickson said, "you might disturb them, so they fly out."

I got as close as I dared. Like so much in Africa, the jagged black lava rock that surrounded the opening was sharp and looked like it would cut. We spent another half-hour exploring until Darsi walked over and suggested we get back into the vehicles. I expected lunch would be ready back at camp.

We travelled north again on roads rich with laterite, dry from rainless skies, and basically untouched. Looking out the window, I started to wonder, would I remember all this? *Could I soak it all up? Was I was ever coming back? Would I get enough photos of the animals for my art?*

Lost in thought, I hardly noticed when we entered a slightly wooded area shaded by acacias. The bright midday sun penetrated the branches and made everything light up. Out of nowhere, an elephant burst on the scene, crossing the road right in front of us. Darsi jammed on the brakes to avoid hitting him. We stared at this magnificent bull, stained red from laterite, hurry across our path, followed by a ball of dust. He took notice of us, but kept going, gliding past us and disappearing into the bush, just as quickly as he had appeared. *That was the close! Lone bulls can be aggressive.*

"Wow! I didn't see that coming," said Darsi, in a matter of fact tone. He looked over his shoulder at us in the back seats. "See, you can't take anything for granted."

"I'm getting that," said Tim.

Back at camp, the usual lunch was waiting: sandwiches with goat's butter, cheeses, a meat of some kind, and sometimes fruit. Not today, though. Here in Tsavo, none was available. After lunch, I went to lie down in my tent. I must have fallen asleep because the next thing I heard was the clatter of pots and pans. *It can't be almost dinner, can it?* I must have lost track of time; late afternoon had crept up on me. I slowly got up and made my way back out into the bright daylight. Groggy but refreshed, I walked over toward a tree to sit in its shade. I caught a glimpse of myself in a shiny pan hanging on a tent pole. I was still puffy in the jaw area. *Ugghh. Was I ever going to have my old face back?*

Half-hidden by the shade, I could become the casual observer. Camp was somewhat empty; most people were probably on an afternoon game run. Ekevu had stayed behind. I watched him for a while as he went about his daily tasks. He hung over the fire and brought it back to a roar, and got food and water off the truck for cooking. His elegant frame moved fluidly from one chore to the next.

It wasn't long before the three Land Rovers came rolling in. From my shady spot, I could see that Tim and Patrick were very animated. Ekevu walked over to them, so I got up, expectantly, as well.

Tim saw me. "Guess what?" he practically shouted.

"I have no idea. What?"

"You are not going to believe it! We saw a leopard!"

"Wow, really? The one time I don't go out!"

"Yeah," said Darsi, "He was relaxing in a tree, before the hunt."

"There is always tomorrow," added Patrick, quietly.

"Yes, no worries," Darsi said in a positive tone. "Let's eat. That will cheer you up."

While sitting around the campfire after dinner that night, a wave of homesickness rolled over me. Sleeping on the ground was losing its charm and I really needed to get re-acquainted with hot running water. I missed the farm, my bedroom, my painting, my family, my pines.

That night, I caught Ekevu staring at me across the fire. For the first time on this safari, he looked serious. As I headed back to my tent for the night, I was hoping another good night's sleep would bring back my enthusiasm for the last day of this safari.

With first light came the voices of a hundred birds, which always inspired me to get up with renewed vigor to greet the day. From our current position, we had a vista to the east where the sun peeked over the horizon, strong and bright. Only a few flattop acacias interrupted the view. Draped in the warm cloak of an African dawn, Ekevu's dark silhouette stood over the fire with the other cooks, boiling chai against a marigold sky. The scent of cinnamon and cardamom was heavy in the air; I walked over.

"Good morning, Miss Hetha. *Habari*," Ekevu said, smiling, as he handed me a cup.

"*Habari*, Ekevu. *Asante sana*."

"Djou are *always* welcome."

Sipping my chai in Tsavo's early glow, the sense that this safari *ndogo* was winding down was almost palpable. Now nearly twenty days in, we only had one more day in Tsavo West. Tomorrow, we would strike out across the even vaster Tsavo East, crossing almost 7,300 square miles on our way to the Mombasa Road, where we would turn north to go back to Nairobi.

By 7 o'clock, most of my fellow travelers were up and moving around. But before they all gathered for breakfast, I had some time to quietly enjoy my chai with Ekevu.

"I love the morning," I murmured. Ekevu took his time in answering as he studied my face.

"I love dat djou love the new day," Ekevu replied. We both turned to look at the sunrise. Then he looked at me with a smile. Before he spoke, he looked pensive for a moment.

"Miss Hetha…"

"Yes?"

"Rememba when djou asked back in Amboseli about what happens to all dis ivory dat dey collect? Ekevu asked.

"Yes. Why?"

"Well, I wanted to tell djou dat de only way to destroy ivory is by *fire*."

I turned my head slowly to look at him, disbelief in my expression. "What?"

"Djes, dey make a bonfire out of it and it turns to dis." He squatted down and scooped up a handful of the red soil. "I am sorry to say, de fire unlocks de ivory's power. Supply stays down and demand stays up."

Ekevu looked up at me. Instead of just dry dirt filtering through his dark African fingers, I saw a savage red earth. I could only think that if Nature is left alone, she is perfection in motion. Her delicate dance needs no partner, least of all human endeavor. I was still processing this as some of my safari mates drifted over to get their chai. Darsi came over and enthusiastically clapped his hands together, as if to snap me out of it.

"Well, today, guys, we are going to tour more of Tsavo West and we are going to visit Kilaguni Lodge while I get us some supplies there. It is one of the oldest lodges built in a park. Hopefully, there will be some elephants to see at the watering holes there."

He turned to Ekevu. "Ready?"

199

"Djes, *bwana*."

"After you guys finish your toast and whatnot, meet me in the vehicles," Darsi added, as he left to talk to Dr. Erickson, while we finished our chai, eggs, and toast.

The day still felt fresh and filled with possibilities. The marigold sky had turned pale blue, and now, as I walked toward the Rovers with Tim and Patrick in my wake, it was bright cobalt. Pulling out of camp, Ekevu pointed out that we were still in the shadow of the Chulyu Hills, and as we got closer to Kilaguni, we might still be able to see Kilimanjaro.

Rocking along the road, once again sandwiched between Tim and Patrick, I was lost in thought. My camera was always at the ready; Tsavo was my last chance to see large wildlife in Africa. Tim must have seen my pensive look.

"So, did you get enough photographs?" he asked, with slight sarcasm. He seemed a touch agitated.

"Um, I think so."

"What are you going to do with all these photos when you get back?"

"Well, I am going to hopefully get them through customs in my lead bag first." Ekevu looked up at me in his rear view mirror. "And then, I am going to figure out how to use them in my paintings."

"Really? How good are you at art?" Tim asked, derisively.

Patrick shot him a look.

"I'm pretty good," I said, not rising to the bait.

Tim smirked and looked out the window.

Patrick put his hand on my knee and smiled. With that, I decided to open up the roof and sit on the tray seat up top. Tsavo's regal and desolate landscape was underscored by distant mountain ranges and accented with the occasional acacia. All alone, these sentinels struck me as great subjects in themselves, a composition ready to paint.

From my rooftop seat, I spotted several Maasai Giraffe. Then, I saw a herd of waterbucks, which practically disappeared against thorny gray underbrush. Impalas stopped to look at us, twitching their big ears. Flocks of vultures circled above us, riding the thermals in the crystal air, while a band of warthogs scurried in front of us, also red with dust.

Following Darsi's Rover, we climbed the single-lane and steep road to Kilaguni. Situated almost 3,000 feet above sea level, it was a third lower in altitude than Nairobi, which made it feel slightly warmer, not unlike our campsite. I got back inside the Rover to get a better look at some rabbit-sized animals sitting on the lava rock walls on the driveway.

"What are those?" I asked Ekevu.

Oh, dey are Rock Hyrax, Miss Hetha. Dey are the closest relative to de elephant."

"Really! Hmmm..."

"Yes, ask Mr. Darsi about dat one."

Guinea fowl scratched in the dust on the path leading to the wide front entrance of the lodge, which led into a promenade of sorts. This, in turn, wound through the lobby and connected to a viewing porch, where the elephants and other wildlife gathered to drink at the man-made pools. Native woods and other materials were used in the interior as well as the exterior of the lodge, giving it an authentic appeal. Like in so much of Africa, creatures from the outside seemed to find their way inside. A colorful lizard scurried across the terra cotta concrete floor and more rock hyraxes sat basking in the sun on the porch walls.

Darsi told us to explore while he and Ekevu gathered what they needed. We all took a minute to watch the elephants by the pools and listen to their low grumblings and other vocalizations. Cape buffalo cautiously approached the water as well, while baboons hung in the background. A herd of zebras eventually made their way over. Even here, the songs of exotic bird calls gave it the feel of being deep in the deepest rainforest.

As usual, Darsi got into an in-depth conversation with the manager of the lodge. Stops like these were the only opportunity we had to find out about current news and events from Nairobi, but Darsi came out smiling as he directed a troop of men carrying crates to his Rover. They packed it so full of food and supplies that he came over to ride with us. Darsi took the driver's seat, while Ekevu was the passenger and the three of us squeezed in the back seat, as usual.

"Ekevu said that these Rock Hyraxes are the closest relative to the elephant?"

"That's right," Darsi said. "They have the same kind of padded feet and number of toes as an elephant. Plus, their incisors are really like little tusks."

For the first time, Ekevu broke from his usual position of wisdom, turned around and with a broad smile said, "I told djou so, Miss Hetha!" I had to laugh.

"So, here is what is going to happen," Darsi continued. "Back at camp, they are already packing up. When we get there, grab your duffles and get back in a Rover." Tim and Patrick looked at Darsi and then at me.

"Already, we're going back?" asked Patrick, tentatively.

"I am afraid so, chap. But we are still going through Tsavo East. We will still see all of Tsavo before it's all over; I promise! The staff is ready to take these new supplies and the Mercedes truck to Mombasa. The truck will meet us in Mombasa. I am putting Ekevu in charge of that, right?"

Ekevu looked at Darsi, "Djes, of course."

Darsi continued, "We'll get you all to Voi by two-ish, and back in Nairobi so you can freshen up, then off to the train station."

Our campsite looked surprisingly empty and lonely. Just as Darsi had said, our stuff was in a pile, waiting to be moved into a vehicle with us. *How did our last lunch in the last park creep up so fast?*

Ekevu walked up behind me after lunch. On his way to hop on the Mercedes truck, he brushed my back with his hand.

"I'll see djou in Mombasa."

"Are you sure?"

He stopped in his tracks, turned around and walked up to me. He stepped in so close, I felt his powerful male energy. "Positive, Miss Hetha. See djou there." He gave me a long look, then winked, turned quickly on his heels and was gone.

Through the dust, I watched as the truck swayed down the road, overloaded and top heavy. I truly hoped that would not be the last time I would see him. I sensed there was more.

We drove south, crossing the Tsavo River, shared by both the east and west sides of the park. After crossing Maneaters Bridge, Tsavo East opened up before us. It was so vast that it seemed devoid of life. Thorny brush camouflaged the inhabitants, like zebras and kongoni, elephants and gerenuks. I photographed a grey-blue Harrier hawk on an old dry dead tree, singular and stark.

Moving southeast, it took several hours to cross all of Tsavo East. As we did, the altitude dropped to a reasonable level, about 1,300 feet. We would exit through the lower part of the park, at the Voi Gate, which was very close to Mombasa Road. On approach, I had to blink to make sure I wasn't dreaming. What rose out of the ground before us was astonishing. It was a bright white modern gas station and restaurant. Like something Frank Lloyd Wright might have designed, it stood there startling and alone against the rough terrain and bright blue skies. So out of place here, it was nothing short of miraculous.

"We're stopping here to refuel," Darsi announced, "and you all can get a snack if you like."

In amazement, Tim, Patrick, and I all looked at each other and before we hopped out. I wasn't particularly hungry, but the boys said they would go in and see what was available. In the meantime, while the vehicles were getting petrol, I just stared at this 21st century structure that made no sense. White, no less. Very optimistic, I thought.

The boys came back with things we hadn't seen in weeks—candy bars! And a can of Coke! Tim got two of each, one for now and the other for Nairobi.

Tim said, "Hey, can you hold this while we go look around?"

"Sure," I said.

He handed me a Coke and a candy bar. They went off and I set the things down behind me on the concrete edge of the island. In this oasis of modernity and normality, it seemed safe enough. I stood around the pumps, looking out onto Mombasa road, thinking about leaving Tsavo. Within minutes, I heard a rustling and crinkling. I turned around to find two male baboons struggling to get into the Coke can and unwrap the candy. Frustrated, one baboon started to bite through the aluminum can and eventually just ran off with it, while the other baboon quickly gave up and shoved the whole chocolate bar down its throat, wrapper and all. He looked at me as if this was standard procedure. *Oh, Lord, what am I going to tell Tim?*

Still surprised, I watched the baboons saunter off. There was no question who ruled this gas station. Soon, the boys wandered back over and Tim immediately reached out for his food.

"Well, you are not going to believe this but..."

"Oh, you didn't eat it, did you?"

"No! No, two baboons just came over and ate your stuff!"

"Yeah, right. Where is it?" he demanded, looking behind me.

"I don't have it. I put it here and they just came over and took it!" I showed him my hands.

"Come on!" Tim was getting visibly irritated.

"I'm serious. I don't have it!"

Dr. Erickson was laughing in the background

and so was Darsi. They already knew about the baboon population here. I guess they forgot to mention it.

"Come on, you two, pick a Rover! We have an Iron Snake to catch!" Darsi opened the driver's door and told Tim to get in front. Patrick and I got in the back. Ekevu, who only stopped to get fuel, had already peeled off onto the road in the Mercedes truck, due south towards the port city of Mombasa. As Darsi pulled out onto the first paved road we'd been on in weeks, driving north, I suddenly felt the pages were turning faster than I could read them. Indeed, a new chapter was upon us. In earnest this time.

CHAPTER TWELVE
Diani Beach ~ Through the Gate

*"The art of art, the glory of expression and the sunshine of the
light of letters, is simplicity."*
~ Walt Whitman ~

Even as the Land Rovers sped through Tsavo's
Voi Gate, they continued to kick up the red earth. The
paved road would allow us to be on the outskirts of
Nairobi in a little over three hours. As we entered the
city, Darsi made the best of wild traffic. It seemed like
another world; a world where motorists played hara-
kiri with their cars.

Closer to the Boulevard Hotel, the smell and
taste of civilization began to resurface. Darsi pulled into
the hotel driveway, and it all came rushing back.

"It seems like we've been away for months, not weeks," Tim remarked. Patrick agreed and I shook my head at the unexpected impact of the city. Conditioned to living with almost nothing, it felt like we had crossed over into another world, but in reverse.

Our respite was small, just enough time to take a shower, get dressed in clean clothes, and meet Dr. Erickson and Darsi back in the lobby to catch the overnight train to Mombasa. In the shower, the last traces of Africa's dust were washed away and the H.P.S. that was crudely inscribed through the layer of dust on my arm was just a memory now. Yes, *maji matumu*, fresh water, was scarce in East Africa. However, her sister, sea water, would be plentiful on the beautiful coral isle of Mombasa. The equator pulled the water from the shower back and forth down the drain. It seemed undecided on which way to turn. But I knew this water lived in Mombasa, and like me, it would find its way there.

The Nairobi Railway Station, built in 1899, was trapped in a time warp. It was hard to tell what century we were in by its architecture and condition. We waited patiently on the sidings to board the Uganda line. In the late afternoon light, steam and dust swirled around the old train. Clearly from the W.W.II era, it looked every bit of its forty-five years.

Finally, we were allowed to board. Once inside, the dark wood trim that adorned the pale cream walls instantly cast me back to another time, another place. The rich interior seemed to resurrect the glory days of British rule. You could easily envision the men and women of this lost era dressed entirely in white, complete with fedoras and wide brimmed hats. The romance of Kenya was alive here; the ghosts hanging in the air. I felt the luxury in the servers, who still used sterling coffee urns, silver utensils, and crisp linen tablecloths. It was in the 4 o'clock tea and the three formal seatings for dinner. Even though this train had seen better days, a glimmer of the Golden Age of East Africa lived on in it. On this day in late July, I felt the weight of history.

In short order, the passengers and the voices of a hundred cultures converged into one train; Indians, Africans, and people from the Middle East were piling in. We apparently had first class tickets, which included a nice berth for sleeping, but third class was without meals and had no berths. At a tenth of the price, third class was overwhelmed. Entire families were boarding, all crammed together. The smells were horrendous and I wondered how sixteen hours with them would look. Thankfully, we were mostly in the dining and sleeper cars.

The Iron Snake slithered slowly out of the station, the engines picking up steam and straining to pull so much weight. Despite all the trials and tribulations that come with living in Africa, I

understood why so many people were drawn to Kenya.
The prospect of making a living here with a plantation
of coffee or tea, turning the soil to grow *kahawa* or *chai*,
was could be an irresistible lure to the adventurer, even
now. There was something magnetic about carving a
life out of land so raw and untouched. I likened it to our
own settlers in the Great American West, who also had
vision and passion. I could see how leaving a legacy in
Africa was the adventure of a lifetime.

It was exciting to watch the scenery as it went
by, faster and faster. It was exhilarating, it felt alive. *I
felt alive!* Staring out the window, I watched the sun set
outside the city limits. The engine's whistle blew as the
train started to pick up speed. It had a forlorn wailing
sound, like the voice of an old warrior at the end of his
last battle.

Traveling three-hundred and thirty miles south
by southeast, we began the long descent towards the
Indian Ocean. Across the lower half of Kenya, it would
be a gradual fall from 5,000 feet to sea level. Soon, the
landscape outside my window would be shrouded in
darkness.

They served dinner late; Tim and Patrick joined
me at a table that was dressed in white linens. Patrick
looked at me often across the table while Tim seemed
lost in thought, in another place.

"Look at this table!" Patrick commented. "You
can almost see yourself in these spoons." He held one

up to the light, and then in front of the candle on the table.

"It's nice to have a proper table set for dinner, isn't it?" I said.

"I should say!" Darsi exclaimed. He had started making rounds to check in with everyone. "How are you making out?" he inquired.

"Oh, fine," I answered.

"Glad to hear it!" he responded. "Keep up the good work." He slapped Patrick on the back and winked at me and Tim.

Dessert was such a treat, and for the first time in weeks, I asked for a glass of cold milk and a cup of hot coffee! After a full meal, I was tired, so I went to bed. Tim and Patrick picked a berth for themselves and I had one to myself. I let the rhythmic clickety-clack of the rails sooth me to sleep. Somewhere deep in the night, our train would cut through Tsavo once again.

All remnants of the bush country had disappeared overnight, and in the morning light, a new array of colors made their debut. As if from the Land of Oz, the dark green, yellow, and shades of chartreuse were so intense and dazzling that they did not seem real. Coconut palms, flame trees, macadamias, and cashew trees grew here; we were almost there.

The railroad tracks crossed over water on as sliver of land called the Makupa Causeway—the last link to the mainland. Even before the Iron Snake started to slow down to a crawl, you could see that the port of Mombasa was a frantically busy place. The second largest city in Kenya, it remains the most exotic center of trade in East Africa.

We slowed down and came to a stop at Mombasa station. Looking out my window, I was reminded of a Caribbean town. Grabbing all our gear, we hurried down the platform where porters and drivers were ready to take our gear and throw it into more Land Rovers.

"*Kwenda*, Likoni Ferry, *asante*," Darsi instructed the drivers.

The only thing holding us back from Diani beach now was Kilindini Harbor. Driving the length of Mombasa took only a few minutes. When we arrived at the dock at the southern end, hundreds of people on foot flooded the ferry as we drove aboard. Many were carrying packages, bundles on their heads; we were caught in a tide of trucks, cars, and human cargo.

I was in a Rover with Darsi."Where is Ekevu?" I asked.

"Not sure. I told him to meet us at a place called Twiga on Diani beach; he knows the spot. I am hoping he is already there."

"I see. But he had such a good head start, though," I remarked.

"He did, but he might have needed to get more supplies in Mombasa city, or gotten held up...you never know in Africa."

Driving south along the coastline was a thrill!
The view of the ocean was still hidden, and the
anticipation was building.

"This is it!" Darsi said, as he pointed to a spot on
our left. "We're here!"

As we jumped out of the Rovers, I still
wondered where Ekevu was. We took our bags off the
vehicles and set them in the shade of the palms.

"Don't look now," Dr. Erickson said. "Here he
comes."

I turned to see the Mercedes truck barreling
down the road towards us. *Yay!* Everyone was pleased
to see Ekevu. He hopped down from the truck and
waved.

"What happened to you?" Darsi exclaimed. "I
thought you'd be here by now."

"Oh, dat is a whole story, Mr. Darsi. Later I will
tell djou..." he smiled. He shook his hand, and Dr.
Erickson's as well. Then he came over to me.

"*Habari*, Miss Hetha!"

"I am glad you made it. I was–"

"I *told* djou I would be back. I do not take
promises lightly," he replied.

"Oh, well, I am glad you are here!"

"Dis place will be good to djou..."

"How so?" I asked.

"Aaahhh, djou will see. *Go!*" He pointed toward the ocean. I nodded and smiled; I was anxious to see what he meant.

I turned to walk towards the water and what lay before me captured my full attention. Curving palms framed a dream-like seascape that would make Paradise blush. The southern edge of Kenya was more than I had imagined; much more.

Once in a great while, someone or something surprises you and completely delights you. Yes, Africa had challenged me and caught me off guard at times, but Diani Beach was pure magic. It seemed as though Providence had brought me to this piece of earth that was impossibly beautiful. The shoreline beckoned to me as the wind caught my hair and the clean air filled my lungs. Hungry for change, I followed the call. Dressed in only khaki shorts and a cream shirt, I started to walk. The powdery white sand met my brown toes and they got acquainted. These first moments out on the beach left me breathless as I absorbed the magnitude of this magnificent coastline. The heat from the sand radiated through my body as this wide, flat beach opened up before me.

Soon, it was only me and this amazing stretch of white wilderness. Like a blank canvas, my body became the only subject, the only form; a singular silhouette casting a long violet shadow in the bright light. As the sun reflected off the sand, blinding white light engulfed me. Peaceful, yet vibrant, it was like a new painting. Like creation itself, this blank space appeared to contain nothing, but for me, it held everything! Full of possibility and freedom, I basked in the apparent nothingness. Fully present in the solitude, a sweet emptiness filled my mind.

As I approached the sea, it was just me and the endless horizon. Gazing east over the ocean, I was endless. On this day, on this beach, I was as infinite as the universe. The rhythm of life was in the pounding of the waves, the heartbeat of the earth. As the cool salt spray hit my face and the wind pinned my shirt against my skin, the sheer force of life coming from this body of water seemed to penetrate my very soul. Foamy white water raced towards me, then retreated. Pulling me in, Paradise and I became one. Yes, Ekevu was right. Just for a moment, the ocean and I were wildly beautiful together.

As I continued walking along the white sand, Diani Beach was leaving an impression on me as surely as I was leaving my impressions on it. Euphoric and free, my feet and my mind wandered. My shallow footprints left a trail in white sand as fine as salt. It was the first time on this adventure I had had a chance to follow the flow and walk alone. Coming from the hostile interior, it seemed like a little slice of heaven. No thorns, no brush, no impediments to walking in a straight line. I could already see how this was going to be the crowned jewel of my time here, and I looked forward to the next five days and nights.

Clear ocean water rushed up to meet me as I continued to walk. It was so transparent and clean, it made my heart leap. The most pristine water I have ever seen, then or since. The suns' rays made the sea sparkle like diamonds on the surface! The ocean's turquoise and aqua greens were only trumped by the cerulean blue of the sky. There was a distinct harmony between the cool water and the intense heat from the sand. But soon, the long afternoon shadows that told me that it was time to turn back.

That first evening, I listened to the seductive sound of palm fronds rustling in the breeze. The hot breath of the tropics surrounded me and caressed my naked skin. Sitting alone on the beach, I watched in awe as the sun kissed the unbroken edge of the earth, turning a palette of blues into shades of tangerine, scarlet, and gold, while the waves relinquished their last touch of jade. Finally, the day faded and the sun melted into the wandering sea. Later, a giant lemon moon smiled down on the earth and made the tides twinkle.

The fire on the beach at dinner was sublime. Equally bright was Ekevu's beaming face. Everyone was relaxed and happy as they acclimated to this tropical utopia.

After dinner, Tim and Patrick wooed me to the waters' edge. *What were they up to?* Soon, it was apparent. Tim stripped his clothes off and quickly ran into the surf; Patrick followed.

"Come on," they shouted, "The water is fantastic!" They did their best to be convincing.

"No, not right now!" I shouted back. They threw up their arms in disgust, their silhouettes backlit by the moon.

When everyone was in their tents and presumably asleep, I quietly crept out, wearing my bathing suit and carrying a towel, and walked up the beach in order to be discrete. When I felt I was alone, I approached the ocean. The waves were calm and gentler at night. The tides pulled me in slowly. The crescent moon lit my way. I waded out, fingertips brushing the shimmering surface. Against the night air, the water felt warm. Once the water was under my ribs, I paused and slowly took off my bathing suit, and let it float on the surface. Catching my breath and closing my eyes, I could easily focus on my body. I leaned back carefully and dipped my hair into the water. Beads of water rolled down my back and dripped off my breasts, glistening in the light of the moon. Isolated in this vast moon glade, I was liberated from all pretense. Released from reality, I lingered in the warm, salty water. Now fully in the seas' embrace, time and I were completely adrift.

Then, I intuitively turned around. Something
had broken the spell. There on the beach stood a figure,
just an outline in the evening light. Whoever it was,
turned quickly and walked away. *How long they had been
watching me and how much had they seen? Was it a
stranger, or someone from camp?* I turned and grabbed for
my suit, now fully aware of my nakedness. I quickly
put my bathing suit back on and returned to the beach.
Arriving at my tent, tired but satisfied, I pulled my
sleeping bag out on the beach. The tropical rhythms of
the night rocked me into a peaceful state. Soon I drifted
into an easy slumber. Except for the constant hum of
insects, all was quiet on the equator.

The cool night turned into another sultry day
with a spectacular sunrise over the ocean. The new
dawn came rolling over the horizon at a pace that

stunned the senses. I sat on the sand overlooking the sea, absorbing the beauty of it all when Ekevu came up behind me, chai in hand.

"Here djou go... "

"Oh, *asante*," I said as I took a sip. "Mmmm... Ekevu, this is so good. What did you do differently?"

"I am not sure. Maybe it is because we are now through *Milango ya Peponi*?" he said. With a sly smile, he clarified, "de Gates of Paradise."

"You're right about that! It is so wonderful here," I sighed.

"And, hurry back to breakfast before all de mangos and papayas are gone!"

"OK," I said. Ekevu smiled.

Back at our rickety wooden table, Darsi showed me how to cut open a papaya and get the seeds out. Ekevu demonstrated how to slice a mango and eat it. Never again would I have such fresh tropical fruit, right from the source!

Just then, Tim stood up suddenly. His cheeks were very flushed; he swayed a bit before he said," I...I...don't feel well..."

He turned and headed to his tent and almost stumbled. Darsi and Dr. Erickson immediately got up and stopped him to feel his forehead.

"Jesus, Tim," Darsi said, "you are burning up! Lay down, son. Come on, in here." They escorted Tim into his tent.

I got up and looked at Ekevu. He looked concerned and followed Darsi and Dr. Erickson to get a sense of his condition.

God, not Tim! What was wrong with him? When Ekevu came out from the tent, I asked him.

"What is going on? Is he OK?"

"Well, we tink he has malaria. "

"*Malaria*? Are you sure?" Then I remembered. He hadn't been taking the prescribed quinine tablets that the rest of us were all taking. His fever skyrocketed to one hundred and five degrees. He was confined to his tent and attended by our camp staff, who kept cold compresses on his chest and head. It seemed ironic. Here Tim was, on fire, when just nine days ago he had survived a grueling trek through ice and snow.

As the morning wore on, anxious for news, I pulled Ekevu aside again. "Is he going to make it?"

"We tink so. He is young and strong. But to make sure, Darsi is going back to Mombasa to get some medicine dat might help. But as djou know, once djou get malaria, it is a lifetime ting."

I chose to believe him but I was still distraught. *So now what?* Even though he was in the best hands under the circumstances, he was in a precarious place.

"Why don't djou take a walk, Miss Hetha. There is nothing djou can do," Ekevu said gently.

I wandered the beach deep in thought. *Was paradise was just an illusion? Was his life at risk? Would we lose someone on this trip after all?*

When I got back, Ekevu waved me over to Tim's tent. Inside, I knelt down beside him. He was delirious and perspiring profusely. I wanted to touch his forehead but instead I softly said, "I wish I could do something for you, Tim." His response was faint, at best. "I am so sorry, Tim. My God, I hope you get better."

After lunch, Darsi gathered us in a circle. "Look, Tim is in good hands now, so we're going to take you to Mombasa as planned. Who wants to go?" Everyone decided to take the opportunity. Ekevu stayed behind.

Darsi was driving with Dr. Erickson in front. After taking the ferry again, we drove two Rovers down Moi Avenue. Lined with coconut palms, it led us into the city and the unforgettable entrance to Mombasa — two sets of giant crossed tusks, one for each side of the street! They harkened back to the days when Mombasa was built on the slave trade, wine, ivory, and animal skins.

In the distance, tall mosque steeples topped with pure gold, heralded a bustling Muslim city with deep roots in the Arab and Persian worlds. Centuries of history were here and it was everywhere you looked. Commerce was alive and well.

"Mombasa was discovered by the Portuguese navigator Vasco da Gama," Darsi remarked, "and we will probably visit Fort Jesus, if we have time, which was the fort that King Philip II of Spain ordered to be built."

"It's called Fort Jesus because from the air, it looks like the shape of a man," Dr. Erickson said, "and it was attacked relentlessly. Eventually, it was just known as 'Island of War'."

"*Kisiwa cha Mvita*," Darsi added, translating the term to Swahili.

We navigated noisy, narrow streets and passed vendors of all types, hawking their wares—fruits, vegetables, cloth, nuts, and more. The streets were designed to be narrow so the buildings would provide natural shade from the sun. Bright white exteriors made with coral concrete reflected the heat and actually sparkled in the strong sunlight. The smells of street food hung heavily in the humid air. From Egyptian falafel to Islamic and Arabic foods; it all made for a heady experience.

Darsi wanted to show us the center of gold trade in Mombasa. When the streets became too narrow and crowded to drive, we walked. I couldn't help but notice strange eyes were on me as we proceeded down a dark alley, deep into the heart of the gold district. Darsi took us to a substantial arched wooden door guarded by some ominous figures dressed in white sarongs and turbans. They stepped out in front of us, blocking our entry. One in particular was very intimidating. He had dreadlocks and looked like Methuselah with a frozen angry expression. They looked me up and down. Darsi didn't seem alarmed, but the hair on the back of my neck bristled. At first, they weren't going to let us pass. Then, reluctantly they opened the door. Inside there were more men with white turbans and draped in white. The atmosphere was dark and heavy with incense. It felt hot and mysterious. Display cases filled with solid gold jewelry filled the room. In 1983, gold was only four hundred dollars an ounce. Buying a gold ring crossed my mind, but I had my piece of Africa, on my wrist.

As we left, many pairs of eyes followed me out. An uneasiness went with me as they glanced at my bracelet. My instincts nudged me along. Dr. Erickson and Darsi must have felt it too; they decided to get back into the Land Rovers and skip Fort Jesus.

Back at camp, I found our wonderful staff continuing to put icy cloths on Tim's forehead, trying to keep him comfortable. I went inside his tent. Kneeling down again, I reached for his hand and squeezed it tight; he squeezed back. His fever was the same, maybe worse. Feelings that I had not been aware of, started to well up. I had come to like him more and more as our journey had progressed, and I couldn't help but admire his spirit.

Trying not to show emotion, I met his eyes. I could see the fear in them. "You're going to be OK. We *are* going to get you back home. I promise." He nodded his head. On impulse, I took my bone ring and put it on his pinky finger.

"Tim…? Tim…," I said trying to get his attention. "Take this. I want you to have it. I will be thinking about you." I don't think he heard my words, he was so sick. I made my exit so he could rest. Something told me that if the tables were turned, he'd be doing the same for me.

The next day, the weather was much like the day before—lovely and ninety degrees with high humidity. Ekevu brought me chai, as usual. Sometimes, without words, we just stood on the sand and savored the intoxicating sea and sky. He would point things out to me and I would listen. I found myself listening with my heart more and more.

"Come on, guys,"Darsi said, "Let's go to this pretty little reserve I know in the Shimba Hills." With only two Rovers, there wasn't enough room for Ekevu, and he had taken a personal interest in making sure Tim was alright, so he didn't mind staying behind. So, the rest of us piled in the Land Rovers again and found our way, on narrow roads packed with red ochre dust, up to an environment of rainforest and grassy hills.

Surrounded by dense vegetation on both sides, the roads took us through acacia groves, deciduous trees, and other scrub until we reached a high point. There, exaggerated hilltops stretched out in three directions. So round, they resembled a naïve painting. Add the giant cycads and borassus palms, whose squat trunks looked too big for their fronds, and you had something that looked like a Dr. Seuss creation. We were dumb-struck; no one had ever seen anything like it.

Even though these hills were only twenty miles from the coast, the elevation gave the breeze from the ocean a cool feel. As I looked to the west, I could barely make it out, but it was there—that giant, Kilimanjaro. To the east was the misty aqua glow of the ocean. *Where else on earth could you watch snow blowing off an extinct volcano in one direction, and turn to see a tropical sea in the other?*

"Keep your eyes open," Dr. Erickson suggested. "Shimba Hills has some incredible species."

"Like what?" Patrick asked.

"Well, for starters, there are over two hundred species of butterflies here and half the rare plants in Kenya."

We remained alert as we wound around shaded roads. Our driver stopped on the edge of a clearing; two species of forest dwellers were grazing. It was the Sable antelope and the Roan antelope, closely related, but different. Each wore its own beautiful rich colors, one primarily black, the other mostly red-brown. Crowned with backward-facing horns and distinctive manes, they were quite a sight. Clinging to their backs were gray ox peckers, also getting a meal.

Because of the thick forest and limited time, we only saw a fraction of the birdlife. But we could hear them! Their songs echoed through the tree canopy, bouncing off the foliage so you couldn't tell where it originated. Dr. Erickson described a few—honey guides, sunbirds, tropical boubous, bulbuls, weavers, tinkerbirds, and turacos, just to name a few.

Then Darsi called out, "Look!"

We snapped our necks to see black and white Colobus monkeys jumping from branch to branch, high in the tree tops. This was one of the few primates we had seen in Kenya besides the baboons and vervets. Driving on, we spotted some large shapes in the shadows. Forest buffalo! A less menacing subspecies of the Cape buffalo, but not as large, Darsi gave it lots of space.

"Dar, let's stop at that gigantic Baobab tree on the way out of here," Dr. Erickson suggested.

"Sure. You've never seen a Baobab this big, guys! These things get big because they live up two thousand years. This one has to be over a thousand!"

"They are known as 'The Tree of Life' because of the cork-like bark, which absorbs water and provides lots of wildlife with food and shelter," Dr. Erickson added. It wasn't long before we came into a shaded area of tranquil forest. In between the trees, the earth looked beaten down. Then I realized there were people living here! In the forest were a few corrugated tin homes and laundry hanging on a line.

"Who lives here?" I asked.

"These are the Mijikenda people from southern Somalia. They escaped to the Kenyan coast because of being attacked by other tribes. The Swahili culture and the Kiswahili language originated with them. Now, they've mixed with the Arab culture to produce what is now one of the Bantu tribes," Darsi explained.

"Very interesting…"

Darsi pulled up in front of this massive tree. I got out of the Rover and went up to take a closer look. It had to be thirty of forty feet around. The way the branches twisted and reached into the air reminded me of old roots. It appeared as if the tree was planted upside down!

While we were standing on this dirt road looking at this great tree, we attracted some little Kenyan children, who must have come out from between the trees. Perhaps Mijikenda, they were full of life and so happy! Their little feet kicked up the dust as they ran over to us. They chattered on in Swahili; they were so excited! It was rare for them to see a white woman with a camera. Dr. Erickson warned me to watch out for them, though. The children here were little pickpockets! And sure enough, very quickly there were an overwhelming number of little hands in the pockets of my khaki shorts. But these children were so sweet and filled with joy, there was nothing to do but to love them. At that moment, I had nothing to give them, though. When we pulled away I gave them a smile, a wave, and said *"Kwa heri!"*

Back at camp, Patrick and I checked in on Tim. He was the same. We came away feeling so helpless. Dr. Erickson said they were doing all they could for him.

"Don't worry. If he doesn't get better soon, we will take him somewhere. His fever is very high, which is concerning us; we are keeping a close eye on him." Dr. Erickson seemed like he had things under control. I had my utmost faith in him...and Darsi.

In the meantime, Darsi thought we might take advantage of our time here. "I'll tell you what. Why don't we go and visit a few resorts along the beach? They won't mind, and they all have pools and bars. I know several." We took a nice walk down the beach with Darsi to explore some.

Dominated by European travelers, it was still a haven for the affluent. First we stopped at The Nomad. Everyone was friendly and hospitable, and they didn't seem to mind that we were not guests. We sat at their outdoor bar, and swimming in their pool was a delightful change from the ocean, which I had been in every day so far.

When we strolled back to camp, Dr. Erickson said there was one thing we could not miss!

"We have to go find some fishermen who have quit for the day and hire them to take us out in their boats so we can see the spectacular sea life here."

"Yeah, those fishermen know this reef better than anyone," Darsi put in. "And, they only charge you a few dollars to take you out so you can snorkel."

"Sounds like fun!" I said.

Patrick was also ready to see what lived below the surface of the Indian Ocean. As luck would have it, we got the attention of two fishermen in a dugout canoe. The smell of nut palm oil penetrated the air as we climbed into their dark mahogany dhow, outfitted with tattered canvas sails. They pushed us out with long poles. Then, while in rhythm with the poling, their melodic African voices broke into song.

"Jambo. Jambo bwana. Habari gani. Mzuri sana.
Wagoni, mwakari bishwa, Kenya yeta. Hakuna matata.
Kenya nchi nzuri. Nchi ya maajabu. Hakuna matata.
Jambo. Jambo, bwana...."

With the backdrop of their hypnotic singing, bright cream sails glowed against an azure sky, clouds billowed up in great masses of white, unfurling before our eyes was a striking and unforgettable panorama. Behind us was the limitless horizon line of the blue-green sea, interrupted only by the vertical mast and poles. *Oh, how beautiful this is!* On the beach, we had

commandeered some snorkel gear. When we dropped over the edge of the boat, we entered another world — the reef! Underneath the surface of the Indian Ocean was a pristine ecosystem so gorgeous it was hard to comprehend. Corals in all colors and shapes dominated the landscape. Barracuda, octopus, sea turtles, and even elusive Whale sharks lived here.

We saw angelfish and butterfly fish swim by like floating striped candy. Coral Trout wore red scales so eye-popping they looked neon. There were spiny lionfish, sea cucumbers with feathery edges, sea urchins, and starfish in every color and pattern rested among the corals. Other creatures just defied classification. I wanted to reach out and touch them all! Totally engaged as I was, the time went quickly. Before anyone knew it, we were heading back to shore. It was difficult to tear myself away.

"How was it, Miss Hetha?" Ekevu asked when we got back.

"Oh, my! I saw things that were I've only seen in Dr. Erickson's lab, or books!" I laughed. "Amazing things live down there!"

"It was crazy," Patrick interjected, "Just crazy!"

"Some of the best snorkeling and scuba diving in the world is right here," Dr. Erickson said. "I am glad we got to see it."

"Hungry?" Ekevu asked everyone.

"Yes!" was the overwhelming answer.

That night, sitting around the fire, we reminisced about our time spent on this coast so far. It was untamed and overwhelmingly beautiful. Undoubtedly, its colors and textures had left a mark on our lives. So far, our paradise was only overshadowed by one thing—*Tim*.

CHAPTER THIRTEEN
Mombasa ~ Into the Fire

"There is in every true woman's heart a spark of heavenly fire,
which lies dormant in the broad daylight of prosperity; but
which kindles up, and beams and blazes in the dark hour of
adversity."
~ Washington Irving ~

For three days and three nights, Tim's life had
been hanging in the balance. Now, on the fourth day, as
quickly as it had come, his fever broke. Looking none
the worse for wear, he emerged from his tent. We were
all glad to have him among us again. Real gratitude
radiated throughout camp. I rushed over to give him a
big hug. Our companion was back! *Oh, thank goodness!*
His strength seemed intact; I felt it in his arms when he
hugged back. Patrick gave him a high-five.

Ekevu looked very happy when he asked him,
"Can I get djou some food, Mr. Tim?"

"Yes, please!" Tim responded eagerly. "Maybe some chai, if you have some left over?"

"But of course." Ekevu went to get it.

"Good to have you back, old chap." Darsi patted Tim on the back. "You probably have a lot of catching up to do, see the sights…"

"Sure do." Tim sighed.

"Well, after some food, let's walk on the beach. Patrick and I will show you Diani!" I suggested.

"You're on!"

Fifteen minutes later, we left camp behind and didn't look back. All three of us took off, running and kicking up the surf in a triumphant sprint. When we caught our breath, Tim put his arm around my shoulder.

"Thanks for being there," he said.

"Oh, you're welcome, Tim. It was the least I could do. I wish I could have done more!"

"I know," said Tim. "What you did was plenty."

We walked a bit further before I mentioned the ring. He glanced at his hands. He hadn't noticed it yet.

"What's this?" he asked, as a smile crept onto his lips.

"Oh, it's one of the bone rings I picked up leaving Nairobi. I wanted you to have it so you knew I was thinking about you."

"You didn't have to do that! You want it back?" he asked.

"No, it's for you to keep,if you like."

"I want you to take it back," he replied. "I insist. It's one of your treasures that you'll be bringing home, remember?" He tenderly took my hand and slipped back on my finger. I was touched.

"Come on!" Tim said, and he started to run again, and Patrick and I chased him up the beach. The waves and the foamy surf of the Indian Ocean cooled our bare toes. It was hard to remember that it was still Africa. Yet, Tim was proof that we were venerable here. Of course, nothing happens suddenly, conditions are always changing. Outcomes are set in motion with the tiniest of actions; as my grandmother used to say, "The devil will take the hindmost."

If there was ever a time when the hindmost was up for grabs, it was this day in 1983. Even with my newly honed instincts, I didn't feel the atmosphere shifting. My small steps in Kenya were about to converge, for better or for worse, at the tipping point. As we walked joyfully along, we were not aware that a stranger had been shadowing us. Following us from a distance, he watched and waited patiently until the right moment. Then, with no warning, he closed in and pounced!

Stepping right up beside me in a grey-green safari outfit, he blurted out, "*Jambo*, Miss. *Jambo?*"

Completely caught off guard, I wheeled around and to face him.

"Excuse me, *vijana miss ya,* I want dat bracelet."
He got in front of me and tried to stop me.

I just stared at him and quickly said, "I'm not
giving it away." Sensing danger, I turned and kept
walking.

He persisted and said, "I'll give you 200
schillings for dat bracelet, Ma'am."

"No thanks…" I said, trailing off as I turned.
"It's not for sale."

"But, Miss, I am de police, Miss. *Askari,* de
police!"

I stopped again. "How do I know that? Do you
have any identification?"

"No, not today." Skeptical, I had heard of
common thieves posing as police, I turned away again.

"Let's go. Now!" I said under my breath to Tim
and Patrick.

Silently, we hurried up the beach. The hair on
the back of my neck was on end now. The "policeman"
seemed to give up, at least for now. Feeling responsible
for my two younger companions, I decided we should
turn around and head back to camp as soon as we
could. First, though, I wanted to create a wide gap
between the stranger and us. So we proceeded north on
Diani Beach, towards Malindi.

"Wow, that was close," Tim sighed. I gave him a
serious glance.

"No kidding!"

Feeling somewhat safe, I stopped for a minute and waded out into the surf, taking deep breaths. Realizing how valuable my bracelet was, I asked Tim to hold it. Wading out further, I let the sea touch the hem of my khaki shorts. Lost in the moment while dangling my hands in the refreshing water, my composure was coming back.

Then suddenly, the sounds of a scuffle and Tim's raised voice jerked me back into reality. He was back! I whipped around to see the same Kenyan man trying to tackle Tim and get the bracelet away from him. He grabbed the back of his shirt, and Tim stumbled but in a flash, he was up and running up the beach. I heard the attacker yell, "*Kuacha, kuacha ... kusubiri !*"

"*Jesus Christ!*" I watched Tim and Patrick take off with this stranger on their heels. In a flash, they were out of sight. With no time to spare, I sprang into action, the adrenaline rushing to meet me as I leapt through the waves back to the beach. I ran like the wind towards camp as my thoughts raced to catch up. I was trying to keep my mind on the task at hand, and I don't know how far I ran or how long it took me. Like in a dream, my legs seemed to be moving in slow motion and I couldn't get them to go any faster. My heart was beating out of my chest and when I charged into camp, sand was flying in all directions. Tagging Dr. Erickson and leaning over, hands on my knees, I tried to catch my breath. Several minutes passed before I was able to say anything.

"Dr. Erickson....Darsi ....ummm, Tim...Patrick, being chased by this guy down the beach....Ahh, I...I...don't know where they went....we better hurry...he's after my bracelet!"

Darsi and Howard looked at each other and I pointed up the beach. We all hurried up the beach.

It was our luck that Darsi knew Diani Beach and its resorts well. He thought that the boys would probably try to find help or refuge in one of the Dutch lodges. He was right, and after poking our heads into one or two lodges, we found them.

Apparently, there was a tussle, Tim had succumbed to the Kenyan man and had had to hand over my bracelet. Darsi, Dr. Erickson, and I rushed into the lobby to find the man behind the welcome desk dialing the rotary phone.

"Hey, bro, what are you doing?" Darsi exclaimed. "What do you think you are doing with her bracelet?"

"It's de police's now. I'm calling de police!"

A distinct feeling of alarm was forming in my chest. Now, Dr. Erickson and Darsi looked concerned, and that put me on high alert.

"I would rethink that," Darsi said slowly and cautiously.

"Too late for dat, Sir," he retorted. Standing in this very open and tropical lobby with the palm leaf ceiling fans twirling above my head, my life was suddenly spiraling out of control. In what seemed like an instant, everything started to unravel. Three policemen burst through the side doors, armed with semi-automatic rifles and loaded down with ammo. They were clearly on a mission. *Oh, God, I wish I could turn back the clock.*

The *askari* grabbed me first, put my hands behind my back, and handcuffed me. Patrick was next, and when Tim resisted, they pushed him to the ground. He hit a coffee table with his shin; the gash it left started to bleed. We were pushed and prodded at gun point into the back of a dark green Land Rover. It was open with no roof, so we sat on metal benches over the wheel wells. The two boys sat on one side and I was sandwiched between two policemen on the other. The third officer started the engine and sped off. It was a stunning turn of events. Speechless, Darsi and Dr. Erickson could only watch as the Kenyan police pulled out of sight and drove us to an unknown destination. At that moment, there was nothing that they could do.

Rattling along in this modified Land Rover, I was in shock at how fast the tides had turned. *How could this be happening? How could they just take us away without Dr. Erickson's permission? We were Americans, for*

God's sake! Didn't that count for anything? We had rights!
Devastated, I stared blankly ahead.

Then I noticed Tim's wound was deeper than I
had first thought. I mouthed 'Are you OK?' Tim
nodded his head. The stare I received from one of the
officers deterred us from any further attempt at
communication. After that, we didn't move or speak.
We kept our heads down, not wanting to provoke them,
and it didn't seem that that would take much.

As we bumped along rough roads, I tried not to
let fear overwhelm me; my head was spinning. *Where on
earth were they taking us? How were Dr. Erickson and
Darcy ever going to find us? Would they ever catch up?
Would we drive into the night? My God, what are they going
to do with us?*

The air was electrified with tension and my senses were being bombarded. The cold metal on my wrists magnified the heat that surrounded us. The smell of perspiration, gas fumes, and dust filled the air. In my ears was the sound of my pounding heart. The policemen were darting their eyes at me, smiling and bantering in Swahili. Perhaps they had never seen an American girl before.

"*Msichana mzuri sana,*" one said. They all laughed. There was that word again.

"*Ndiyo..... uzuri,*" another smirked. It was clear that I was the topic of conversation. This was a layer of attention I wasn't counting on and did not welcome. Ideas were surfacing now that I had never confronted before. *What did they really have in mind for me? Was this an arrest, or kidnap?* I searched my companions' faces for a sign, anything that would give me answers. They were just as lost.

As we drove on, minutes turned into an eternity. The roads went from bad to worse. The heat and the humidity were intense. I noticed that we had continued to climb slowly upward. Eventually, we entered a dark jungle filled with mostly palms. The winding road brought us out into a small clearing, where there sat a primitive, one-story cinder block structure. Remote and hidden, it was a virtual needle in a haystack. The only distinguishing feature was a small break in the tree canopy where the sun came down in shafts and highlighted the crude stucco exterior. The few tiny windows that I could see had bars on them. That feeling of tightness was growing in my chest again. My heart continued to pound in my ears as my mind reeled. *How in the hell are they ever going to find me?*

"*Kupata nje!*" One officer sneered, as we came to a halt. We all stared at him blankly.

"Get out!" he shouted.

We quickly obliged and hopped off the back of the Land Rover. They escorted us into this simple building, that clearly had no electricity or running water. As they lined us up in the hallway, I glanced at the cells. My future looked dismal.

Then, seemingly incongruent with the situation, they asked us if we wanted a Coke? A Coke? *What?* Trust of any kind had flown out the window for me an hour ago. I refused, thinking they might try to add a sedative, a drug, or even poison. Holding my breath, I watched as Tim and Patrick accepted and drank theirs. So far, they seemed fine.

Mumbling in Swahili amongst themselves, they left momentarily and came back with a woman officer. Dressed in the same grey-green uniform, she took of my handcuffs, then ushered me into a small room and closed the door. The room was completely empty; blank. I stood motionless as she took off my bone ring and put it in her pocket.

Then, in English she said, "Unbutton your blouse, honey." Stunned by hearing my native tongue coming from her mouth, I simply responded and did as she requested. She reached inside my bra and felt around my breasts for other objects.

Then she said, "Take off de pants, and de underwear."

Blind-sided once again, I stammered, "Wh..aa..t?"

She repeated herself, this time louder. I hesitated. *Where was this all leading?* My khaki shorts fell to the floor and I pulled down my panties just enough so she could explore between my legs. I held my breath and waited for her to penetrate my vagina and search around. Thankfully, she didn't. I put my clothes back on. She opened the door and ushered me back into the corridor and across the hall to another room. There was a growing sense of doom in this new room, also dark and oppressive. The dark wooden desk sat next to a few primitive chairs. Light from one tiny window broke through the shadows. The only warmth came from a single candle burning on the desk. Its glow was just enough light to reveal some scattered papers on the desk and some hastily painted walls, stucco missing from bullet holes. She told me to sit down and proceeded to ask me some questions.

"Where did djou get dat ivory bracelet, Miss?"

"I....I....traded old jeans for it back in Nairobi," I replied. "The Maasai told me it was bone."

"I see," she said as she scribbled some things down on a piece of paper. "Were you going to sell it?"

"No!"

"Were djou going to take it out of dis country?"

"Umm, well, I didn't know what it was, for sure," I said reluctantly. *Was this going to be my official statement?* She proceeded to ask me a few more questions. Afraid and unsure, I found myself handing over my destiny by simply telling the truth. I was too numb to try to make anything up. Now on record for perpetuity with things that were incriminating, my mind raced. *What on earth would the penalty be?* I stared at the orange flame, flickering alone in the blackness. I felt the numbness growing. Then, the female officer blew out the candle and the room went black.

She took me back into the corridor and then, along with Tim and Patrick, out into a courtyard attached to the back of the jail. Becoming more volatile by the moment, the atmosphere kept shifting. The walls were about seven feet high, cinder block, and roughly covered in stucco. The three officers who carried rifles lined us up against the back wall. Then, standing back about twenty feet, they stood directly in front of us.

Since I didn't have handcuffs on anymore, one officer told me to put my hands behind my head. There was a long pause. *What were they waiting for?* I wasn't sure. But then, in the silence, it suddenly dawned on me what could be next. Cold fear was rising out of the pit of my stomach as they held their rifles in front of them. *Were they waiting to shoulder their machine guns, point them at our heads and pull the trigger?*

CHAPTER FOURTEEN
Uwazi ~ The Thin Veil

"The best way out is always through."
~ Robert Frost ~

As they stared at us with guns at the ready, a chill went through my body. So, this was how it was going end for me, with an executioner's bullet? I had so much of life ahead! *Was this my time to go?* I wasn't ready. The warrior in me started to look for a way out. Like an animal, I wanted to explode and escape. *Could I make it over the wall? I was a fast runner. Maybe I could cause a distraction and run?* My heart was pounding again. My body was on a hairpin trigger. *Maybe I could get around these guys. But, was it worth the risk?* I knew if I tried to escape, they wouldn't hesitate, they would shoot to kill. My life would end here, bleeding to death in a remote jungle.

Motionless and frozen with terror, there I stood. The transparent veil was right in front of me now. I felt my world would shatter at any moment. *Would I be protected from the other side?* As the seconds dragged on… tick, tock, tick, tock… warm sunshine filtered through the trees and hit my face. It threw long shadows behind us on the wall. *Were these my final moments? Was every minute that passed my last? My God, where are you, Dr. Erickson? Please, please find us, hurry!* The suspense was crushing.

Then, abruptly and without ceremony, they motioned us back inside. Taking a deep breath, I realized I had faced my mortality once again. We were going to get another chance.

Once inside, we were split up. Tim and Patrick's handcuffs were removed and they were taken to a cell, while I was put in a cell across the hall. The door slammed. I was locked inside four walls, which were discolored and dreary. The cement floor was broken up by puddles of urine and unknown stains. In this hellish place, the only feature was the one source of light—a small window with bars on the back wall. In the corner of this six–by–nine–foot cell, under this only source of light, were five Maasai women, crouched in the corner. Wearing traditional red *shuka* and beaded yokes, they smelled of sour goat's milk, and looked forlorn and thin. Like cornered animals, they huddled together. Except, this cell wasn't good enough for animals.

My new reality was so overwhelming; I found it hard to focus. I couldn't imagine what Dr. Erickson and Darsi were thinking after the police vehicle took us away. They were facing their own set of uncertainties.

"Damn it!" Darsi exclaimed, as the police pulled away from the resort. "God, this is the last thing I wanted to happen!"

"Now what?" Dr. Erickson asked.

"Oh, bloody hell, I don't know! We have to find them first. Let me think." They walked back through the lobby and hurried down the beach. By the time they got to camp, Darsi had a direction.

"OK, Howard, there are only a few jails here in Mombasa; we'll just have to narrow it down!"

Ekevu and the other campers were anxious for news. "Where are dey? Why aren't dey with djou?" Ekevu's asked, slightly panicked.

"They got frickin' arrested!" Darsi exclaimed. Everyone gasped. "And, we have no idea where the police took them!"

"Djou...are serious? Ekevu stammered.

"I'm afraid so," Darsi replied.

"*Mungu wangu,*" Ekevu whispered.

People wanted to help; Darsi put his hand up. "I'm sorry, too many cooks in the kitchen. I'm going to call on some of my friends in Nairobi, see what we can do."

"Let's all take a deep breath. We have two days to get them out before we leave for Amsterdam," Dr. Erickson assured everyone. Darsi gave Dr. Erickson a quick glance, then pulled him aside so no one could overhear him.

"Howard, you don't understand. Moi just reinstated the Detain Without Cause law, this year!" Darsi explained. "Thanks to last year's uprising, nothing is a guarantee." They both turned back towards the campers, who were all waiting for some scrap of hope.

"What can I do, Mr. Darsi?" Ekevu asked.

"Nothing."

"Can I come with djou?"

"No. Not now. I need to leave someone here in charge of these guys." Darsi waved his arm toward the camp. "We better get going now, we have our work cut out for us," Darsi announced. "And don't wait for us." Darsi and Dr. Erickson hopped into the nearest Land Cruiser and took off.

"She is going to be fine."Ekevu said, mustering his most convincing delivery to anyone who was listening. Then, he turned and sat against the trunk of a palm in the shade.

In the jail cell, I leaned my back up against a clean space in the wall, tilted my head back and closed my eyes. Oh, if my family could see me now, they wouldn't believe it! *Just let me survive.* I was trying not to let a wave of panic overtake me again, but my brain kept pumping thought after thought. *What had I done? Why didn't I just get rid of that bracelet? Why didn't I just give it to the police?* Now caught in a web of paralyzing thoughts, I tried to break free. *Was I ever going to see the United States again? Would they decide to shoot me after all? How would I ever get in touch with my parents? Would anyone bring me food and water?* Unsuccessful, I hung there, trapped.

Eventually, I surrendered myself to the inevitable. I was completely vulnerable, and fighting it seemed futile. Resigning myself to whatever was next, I slid down the wall onto my haunches and put my head in my hands. The Maasai women must have wondered what a young white woman was doing in a place like this. I was wondering, too. Still shaking off the overwhelming feeling of misfortune, I went over and asked them in English why they were here. They understood, and answered in English, which they actually spoke quite well, and a few shared their story, the same for all five of them. Their crime was simple — they had disobeyed their husbands, and that is punishable with imprisonment in Kenya. Hearing this, there seemed little hope for me.

I went back to my spot against the wall, and gazed at the small window of the cell. I wondered what time it was, and I started thinking of my precious bedroom window back home. *Oh, how I missed the mimosa tree!* The joy it brought me when I climbed its branches, and the sweet smell of nectar that came from its fuzzy pink blossoms. I thought of all the butterflies and bees that came to visit every day. I wish I was there now! This was unbelievable. Tears started to pour down my cheeks. I tried to stop them, but it was like trying to stop the grains of sand in an hour glass. As minutes slipped into hours, hope seemed like a ghost.

Then, out of nowhere, Tim's voice came across the hallway. "Are you O.K.?"

Hopping up bravely, "Oh, yeah, I'm OK. How about you?"

"Sure, we're fine," he answered.

The sound of footsteps cut our conversation short. It was comforting to have the boys across the hall. I imagined Tim was seeing this as an adventure of a lifetime and not a real threat. Nonetheless, if I ever got out, apologies to him and Patrick would be in order.

How much longer would we be here? Where are Darsi and Dr. Erickson? In my despair, I remembered my grandfather, Colonel Arthur Lee Shreve II. He served in both world wars and was a Colonel in W.W.II. He spent four years as a prisoner of war, captured at Bataan in the Pacific theatre. However, he did survive. Maybe there was a chance for redemption after all.

As the hours passed, no one came to see the Maasai women. No one brought food or water for any of us. What made this all the more sad was that once I was gone, one way or another, those women might still be there, and more would take their place.

The sunlight coming through my cell window had shifted quite a bit. Time kept slipping through my fingers. As every minute passed, I felt my chances of getting on that flight to Amsterdam were farther away. Carefully, I paced a small section of the floor of my cell. As nightfall approached, I was dreading the possibility of spending it here, in these conditions.

CHAPTER FIFTEEN

Ukombozi ~ The Final Question

"It is not light that we need, but fire; it is not the gentle shower, but thunder. We need the storm, the whirlwind, and the earthquake."
~ Frederick Douglass ~

While thinking about my new position in life and what the night would bring, I heard the faint sound of a voice that was not Kenyan. On tiptoe, I tried to look out my cell door. I couldn't see anything. I listened harder. *Could it be? Was that Darsi's voice? Yes! It was! Oh, thank God!* I could hear Dr. Erickson's voice too. I couldn't make out what they were saying, but the tone was serious, and they went on for about fifteen minutes.

Just before this, Darsi had burst into the building and immediately asked the first officer he saw,

"Are you holding three American kids here? We're looking for them."

"Djes. Who are djou?" inquired the officer.

"My name is Darsi and this is Dr. Erickson from the United States. For goodness sakes, bro, these are just tourists! *Kids!*"

Another uniformed Kenyan came forward. "I am in charge here."

"Look," Darsi said, stepping in very close to this supervisor, "it was a mistake. They are not smugglers. What's it going to take to work this out so everyone looks good?"

"We are not inclined to let dem go, Mr...?"

"Ruysenaar," Darsi supplied.

"Especially, not de girl."

"Listen, am I going to have to call the American Embassy or just talk to the people who are in charge of you?" Darsi pointed at the officer's chest. "This is going to cause a stir, and isn't going to look good for Kenya."

"A country that depends on tourism," Dr. Erickson added.

The supervisor considered it for a moment, and then spoke. "We will let her go, as well as de boys. But we are going to hold her passport and, in the next few weeks, she will have to go to trial here."

"In the next few weeks! " Darsi practically shouted. "No, no...you don't understand; they are leaving for the states the day after tomorrow!

How...*what*... do we need to do, bro, to make this happen?"

"We might be able to work dis out," the supervisor answered, "Come with me." They went into the same room where they took my statement and closed the door.

I could hear the voices, but it wasn't until much later that I learned what had been said. All I knew right then was that shortly after the voices stopped, the sound of their footsteps echoing on the concrete and started to come closer. Then the rattle of keys, the door opened. I was free! A wave of relief rolled over me. When I saw Darsi and Dr. Erickson, I rushed to hug them. It was incredible how happy I was to see them!

Darsi pulled me aside. "Heather, listen, they are going to let you go but there are a few conditions."

The officer explained them to me, "We will let djou go, and the boys, but we are going to hold de passport so djou cannot leave the country. Djou will go to trial tomorrow in de Shimba Hills and there, dey will decide if djou are guilty or not."

Darsi shot the man a glance and said, "We will be back as soon as we can with her passport."

"Fine, sir," the supervising officer nodded.

Darsi and Dr. Erickson hurried us back to camp, where I grabbed some water, a bathroom break, and my passport, and jumped back into the vehicle. As soon as that passport left my hands, I felt Fate right beside me, again.

As we returned to the camp and settled into Twiga that night, I apologized to Tim and Patrick for entangling them. Ekevu wanted to know everything. But I was so tired, I put my sleeping bag on the beach and fell right to sleep.

I awoke the next day to another spectacular sunrise on the beach. Then I remembered. Not only was it the last sunrise I would see here but I would spend most of it in uncertainty. My fellow campers tried to assure me that it would all work out. Unfortunately, they really didn't know that my future was twisting in the wind. All my faith was in Darsi and his thirty years of living in Kenya. Really, I was still on God's good humor.

About mid-morning, Darsi came to get me. "Let's get going, Heather. I expect that you are not the only one going to court today and we don't want to be late; everything takes longer in Africa." He smiled. "Why don't you go and hop in that vehicle over there?"

Dr. Erickson and I got into one of the Land Cruisers and waited. I saw Ekevu walk up to Darsi.

"I want to be there," Ekevu said.

"Well, I am not sure this is going to be—"

"Please," Ekevu said quietly.

"OK, sure. You can drive," Darsi surrendered.

Somehow the trip into the Shimba Hills didn't seem quite as long. The roads were just as awful, though. The courthouse was another one-story, primitive, cinderblock building. This time, covered in pink stucco. Sunlight filtered through the forest canopy and dappled the velvety pink walls. I noticed the air this time. It was fresh from all the oxygen coming from the trees and from the breeze off the ocean. The courthouse had tall shuttered doors and windows, all open. I could hear the hum of many Swahili voices coming from inside. Outside, there was just as much activity. A line of Kenyans, men and women, came out one side door and wrapped around the whole building. They were all waiting to see a judge. To me, it was just a cornucopia of bright colors as I looked at all these people from all walks of life, adorned in native clothes and beads.

I wondered what this long line meant for me. *A long wait, or something else?* Darsi told us to stand still while he squeezed his way past lots of dark faces and through a side door. He took Ekevu with him. *What was he up to?* I was surprisingly calm; it was out of my hands. Looking around, police were everywhere. It appeared that the other defendants were being treated fairly and in an orderly fashion.

Darsi came back out and said, "OK, Heather, they're going to let us get in here and be seated so you can get before a judge sooner rather than later."

257

"Thank goodness," I said. Dr. Erickson looked relieved too.

"Where is Ekevu?" I asked looking behind Darsi.

"Oh, he went…to… uh, I guess he is still in there." Darsi looked back inside the crowded doorway.

Inside the courthouse, despite the open windows and doors, it was steamy and hot. The air was thick with the odor of unwashed bodies and that ever-present smell of sour goat's milk. The room was filled with rows of pews, filled to capacity. We squeezed our way into one, and I wedged myself between Darsi and Dr. Erickson. Ekevu was still nowhere to be seen. The mood was tense now, as the unknown was looming in front of me once again.

I turned to Darsi, nervously. "Darsi, what's next? What should I say once I get up there?"

"Well, here's the thing," he began. "They are going to read the charges to you and ask you if you are innocent or guilty. Just plead guilty, because if you say you are innocent, they will accuse you of lying and put you back in jail."

I looked at him incredulously. "You mean… *are you sure?*"

"Yes, I'm sure," he answered. "There was a European couple two weeks ago who pleaded innocent to having ivory and they put them in jail for two weeks. Hopefully, they will just fine you and let you go."

To me this looked like an impossible situation.

"But I am almost out of money?"

"That's fine," he said. "We'll cover you." I just looked at him. I'm sure he could see the concern and fear in my face. *Would I stay, or would I go?* This was the final question. The severity of the situation was starting to sink in. I started to question my plea. Follow Darsi's advice and take a chance? Or plead innocent. *Where was that Ekevu?* I wanted so much to ask him what he thought. Ekevu always had my back. But then, so did Darsi.

The courthouse building had no electricity or telephones. Without ceiling fans, it was getting hotter and hotter. From what I could see, at the front of the courtroom sat three men, presumably judges. Each one had a table, some paperwork, and a gavel in front of him. So simple and so primitive, and yet here I was— dangling over the edge, waiting for those three judges to determine my fate.

As the minutes dragged on, my life started to feel strangely empty. *What had it all been about?* I struggled, trying not to let irrational thoughts chase away logic. I tried to focus, but my thoughts became as scattered as the white petals underneath the apple trees back home. It seemed to be getting hotter by the second. Wishing this was all behind me, I checked with Darsi again.

"Are you sure I should plead guilty? What if they just want to prove a point or they just don't like Americans?"

Looking at me with a steady gaze, he said, "Trust me."

I was getting more scared the longer I waited. I scanned the room, looking and listening for any sign, anything that would give me a clue as to my likely outcome. The judges were stoic, and spoke in Swahili, which made it almost impossible to read the atmosphere. As time went on, the pressure seemed to increase. My mind started to become slightly unhinged. My thoughts, as scattered as the white petals under the apple trees back home.

Then finally, they called my name. I was up. No more time to dwell on possible outcomes. Walking to the front of the room and standing before these three Kenyan judges was like playing poker, accept I already knew who held the better hand. Out of the corner of my eye, I could see the police standing there…waiting. My heart was pounding again. One of the judges read the charges.

"Illegal possession of ivory…" The sound of my heart beating was all I heard; my mind was frozen. I blanked out for a moment. Then I heard, "How do you plead?"

I snapped back to the present and regained my

composure. Without thinking, I said, "Guilty, your Honor."

"Guilty, as charged," he bellowed. The crack of his gavel hitting the wood desk made me jump. "We are fining djou 800 schillings. Djou are free to go, here is your passport. But djou may not return to dis country, Miss."

Turning away with passport in hand, the world seemed to lift from my shoulders. I was in a daze as I walked back to my seat. A fine of $300.USD and a criminal record in Kenya seemed like a small price to pay for liberty.

Swiftly, Darsi and Dr. Erickson escorted me out the back of the courthouse through shuttered doors. And there was Ekevu, leaning up against the doorway, waiting patiently. He beamed as the tropical light flooded in from behind him, his smile just as bright. I smiled back, but with a heavy heart. Ekevu, comforting as always, put his arm around my shoulders briefly as we walked to the vehicles. Being banned from Kenya was a sobering thought and an unexpected twist. It was a quiet ride back to camp.

Around the campfire that night, the atmosphere was very different from other nights around the fire. Everyone was focused on getting back to Maryland in one piece. Just one more night in Africa; one more night to soak up paradise before we returned to Nairobi.

The next morning, we broke camp for the last time. We packed and loaded our tents, food, and gear. Ekevu brought my final cup of chai to me on the beach. He was not his normal beaming self.

At the station in Mombasa, we had a chance to say farewell to all of the wonderful drivers and porters. I knew this would be the last time I would see Ekevu. When we were ready to board the train, he walked over to me, smiling again.

He stood in the late afternoon African sun, his dark skin glowing against his white shirt. All the times we'd spent admiring nature came flooding back all at once. He hesitated, then pulled me to him and hugged me tight. He whispering in my ear, "*Kwa heri*, Miss Hetha... *wewe ni uzuri*."

I looked at him and smiled.

"Good-bye, Hetha Shreve; djou *are* a beauty."

Tears began to well up in my eyes.

"Thank you, Ekevu. Thank you…for everything." He stepped back, still holding my arms.

"I am sorry to see djou go but, I am glad djou *can* go home." He smiled half-heartedly, his eyes were glassy.

"I'll miss you," I said.

"Me, too," he said quietly.

Before I could turn away, he said, "Hetha, rememba… "

"What?" I whispered.

"Noting, *noting*…" His voice was charged with emotion.

Slowly, he finally let me go and I turned to walk down the sidings to board the train. I paused at the train car steps. Turning around to wave to the camp staff and Ekevu one more time, I saw that Ekevu was already gone. My heart sank.

"Good-bye! *Asante!*" I yelled to everyone who remained. *"Asante sana…"* My words seemed grossly inadequate in comparison to what they had given to me.

I climbed the steps and the engine began to move off, late, as usual. Once inside, it seemed everyone else's spirits were up. We had a roof over our heads, a semblance of a bed, and hot food at a table, but it all seemed of little consequence now.

A quiet sadness followed me aboard. Yes, I was free and homeward bound, but at that moment, it seemed there was only my brown skin, a tired body, and photographs to show for my extraordinary journey. In comparison to what I had lived, it seemed so hollow. I didn't want it to be all gone.

The Iron Snake made her way back through the savage and beautiful interior, over the Tsavo River and through it all. When I awoke the next morning, Mombasa was gone as well. We were back to a dry and relatively dull landscape. Then, near the outskirts of Nairobi, we passed the second largest slum in Africa – Kibera. The railway tracks are the southeast border to one million people slammed together in less than a square mile. In every direction were tin roofs and cardboard walls. A shanty town on a massive scale, it holds a heart breaking one-quarter of Nairobi's population. Everywhere, children were starving, some crippled, and others so sick. Seeing the skeletal Ethiopians coming over the border in northern Kenya was enough; this was too much. And here I was, on a luxury trip by their standards, passing them by, and there was nothing I could do. That moment, as with so many others recently, became a defining one. I realized it was time. I was ready; ready to go home.

CHAPTER SIXTEEN

Home ~ Follow the Swallows

"There are two ways of spreading light: to be the candle or the
mirror that reflects it."
~ Edith Wharton ~

I may have left Africa with a heavy heart,
leaving behind people and places that had made me
feel more alive than I ever had been, but when I reached
American skies, my spirit soared. July 21, 1983, the day
I climbed down the airplane steps and walked across
the tarmac of JFK airport, was a day I thought I would
never see. It didn't matter that the flight from
Amsterdam to New York seemed to last a lifetime or
that foreign bacteria from the food was finally catching
up with me. It wasn't important that I had just traded in

the clear, clean air of Africa for the polluted air of
Manhattan, or that I was still not well-rested or dust
free. I was safe! It was everything that I had hoping for;
home and America at last!

When the bus from JFK arrived back in
Maryland, it was with the very extraordinary people
who had been with me for almost a month. Saying
good-bye was very difficult, especially to Tim and
Patrick. If I had known I would never see any of them
again, accept for Dr. Erickson, I don't know that I could
have said good-bye to them at all.

Everything on the farm was exactly how I left it.
The barn swallows still swooped and chirped, the
mimosa tree was still outside my bedroom window,
and my dog Dash remembered me. Little had changed.
But as the stories started to roll off my tongue with
family and friends, I realized that wasn't true at all. It
took weeks for my parents and sister to absorb what

had happened in Kenya because it was so disconnected from life in America.

I got all fifteen rolls of film home safely and had them developed. I reacquainted myself with my art and watercolors, which I missed so much. I walked the farm in a trance, still reeling with memories.

It was at that opportune moment that I reached out and met George Small. Sometimes, all we really want is to have a witness to our lives; someone who can vouch for our journey. In the case of my African experience, that is what George Small was for me.

When I reminisced with George at his dining room table in Baltimore, it didn't seem like a distant dream anymore. George had seen much more of what I had seen, heard more of what I had heard, and lived a good part of the last dozen years in Kenya. His experiences with the wilderness had given him a deep wisdom, which was affirming and enlightening to me. George became the only person I knew who really understood my story of East Africa. What we shared was that rush of emotion Africa brings to your heart. He was the anchor that helped me make sense of it all. For us, it was understood—when God created East Africa, He created a masterpiece, and we were the ones honored to see it.

George was a tall, deceivingly quiet, intelligent, and big-hearted man who was forty years older than me. Unlike me, George hadn't chosen East Africa, East

Africa had found him. Sam Small, George's older
brother, bought a forty thousand acre ranch in Kenya in
1952. They called it *Mpala*, and it was thrust upon
George in 1969, after Sam died of a heart attack sitting
in a rocking chair on the front veranda. Without a wife
and children, Mpala became George's alone. Over time,
he grew to love the ranch and the country around it. He
was at peace with the rhythms of the land and the
energy of the equator. He was tuned in to the
indigenous peoples—the Kikuyu, the Samburu, and the
Maasai. He appreciated the animals and the beauty they
brought, and the danger. Like the continent itself, the
stories he carried around with him were immense.
George Small was infamous; at least in Baltimore.

    His ranch took up a sizable part of the northern
region of Kenya known as Laikipia, just south of
Samburu. George would spend months away from
Baltimore on Mpala. In this raw landscape, it was hard
to see how he managed to have a full-fledged cattle
ranch, but he did. He carved a life out of the rocks and
the acacia bushes for his cattle in a place where water
was a luxury.

    Despite the terrain and the inconveniences of
rustic living, people loved to visit George there. "Yes, I
have visitors there all the time," he told me. "I have
room for at least ten people, give or take. People seem
to love it."

I knew he was generous with his ranch and with his time, and the warnings of the inherent dangers didn't seem to repel anyone. Tale after tale would roll off George's tongue. One in particular I can recall very well.

"I remember one night," mused George, "and I know you will understand this. I always told people to stay close to the house in the early morning and at dusk. As you well know, that is the time you can be lion bait or attract a Cape buffalo! One time there was a visitor, a man, who decided to take an evening stroll anyway. He left the safety of the grounds and, sure enough, a Cape buffalo bull spotted him in the bush. You know, when bulls are alone, there is no such thing as a 'mock' charge. So, this bull gave chase and the guy turned and ran and found the nearest acacia tree. Sadly, the tree was really a bush and it wasn't tall enough. His feet were still within reach. So what did that tenacious Cape buffalo do? He proceeded to methodically use his sharp, rough tongue to lick through the bottom of his shoe, through his flesh, right down to the bone! I think after that, guests paid attention to me," George smiled.

For me, it just brought back memories of what I narrowly escaped in Samburu myself. It showed me again that it was probably good that I had gone into Kenya "blind."

Because George didn't have any children, I think he did his best to give his time to the youth he met along the way. He was generous enough to offer me and some other local teenagers the opportunity to visit his home in Ontario, Canada in September, 1983. It was a rustic retreat nestled atop one of the rocky islands in the Thousand Islands region of the St. Lawrence River. Only accessible by pontoon plane and boat, it had the added luxury of electricity, running water, tennis courts, and extra guest cottages. We soaked up the September sun and George's stories for about a week. George was only in my life for a season but that was more than enough.

One night back in Baltimore, George turned to me and said in his unassuming way, "What if you were to paint something for me, maybe of Mpala?"

"Sure," I said. "What did you have in mind?'

"Oh, I don't know. Maybe a typical landscape with a Cape buffalo in it?" he smiled, "You'll help me decide?" I was happy to oblige. Besides, his company and his stories were some of the most entertaining I'd ever heard.

As we waited for the butler to serve our dinner, I looked around the room. It was filled with dark wood antiques, clearly from generations past that could tell their own stories; maybe even some that had come from Africa. Dimly lit, the only source of light was two wall sconces and the glow of candlelight from tall tapers on the table. Staring into the flickering flames, I was drawn in by their fire. I was caught again, magnetized to a place that showed me the essence of life and began a process of transformation. Subtle at times, sometimes we see the metamorphosis, and sometimes our awareness comes later. Somehow, people drift in and out of your life at exactly the right moment. I will never know how the bargaining for my release really unfolded, or how many people beyond Darsi and Dr. Erickson played a part. I will never know if my arrest was a random act or a set-up, or even if my bracelet was really ivory. I will never know who was on the beach that night in the moonlight. Sometimes the not knowing is the gift.

Much later in life, the real ending of my story would emerge. Twenty-seven years would pass before I would learn that a simple bribe had set me free. One hundred USD was paid to the Kenyan police under the table to ensure my freedom. Almost thirty years would pass before I knew what a boiling caldron of corruption the Kenyan government was in 1983, and the extent of the dangers we had faced. At the time, I was simply – and blissfully – in the dark.

But now I see. Now I see that sometimes we are bold and arrogant enough to think that we can plan and control every part of our lives, or even find our purpose. In truth, purpose is crafted on the anvil of life; it finds us. And now I see that my inner light has now become my outer incandescence and that the portrait of my life has developed just as it should; colorful, strong and bright.

Looking back, I didn't understand my position in the wilderness or even the world. Dwelling in the wild places gave me something I couldn't touch. Three simple questions; *Who are you? What do you stand for? How far will you go?* I had already begun the safari of my life, one day at a time, one question at a time. Eventually, they would all be answered. In truth, I left with *everything* that I would ever need.

Now, when I look at a Mimosa tree, I see it for what it **is**—an acacia. When I see a barn swallow, it means home. Not just as a place, but a journey to the light, where a flame lives that can't be altered by your circumstances or your surroundings. And whenever I am in a coffee shop and they ask me what kind of brew I want, "Kenyan, please," is always my answer. Then I smile to myself. *If they only knew.*

Years later, folded and stuffed in my safari
jacket pocket, I found this.

Dear Heather,
Life is a beautiful
river; rest on her
banks and you will
see yourself in
her waters.
Watch the river—
She always gets
where she is going
and is happy on
the way; sit with
her enough, you
will find your
flow ... I know you will—

kwa heri,
Ekevu

The unexpected is always upon us.
That's what Kenya gave to me—
an unexpected gift.

273

Yes, I remember Africa…

I remember everything-the smell of swirling acrid dust and fragrant wood smoke curling in cool air. I can still hear the rhythms- the haunting hum of the Maasai warriors chanting, the crescendo of insects at night, the thunder of a ten thousand hooves, the whirr of a million wings and the melodic voices of fishermen, the sound of Ekevu's voice. I still remember the taste of raw gazelle flesh and sour goat's milk. I can still see all the colors- the whites of Kilimanjaro, the aqua green sea, the reflection of the lemon moon, the blood red earth of Tsavo, and the final orange fire on the horizon. I can still feel the burn of the sun on my dusty skin, the dryness of thirst… the weight of my ivory bracelet. But, above all, I remember a sense of terror… and how it feels to have people watching over you.

Yes, I remember… and I'll **never** forget.

EPILOGUE

"Excellence is an art won by training and habituation. We do not act rightly because we have virtue or excellence, but we rather have those because we have acted rightly. We are what we repeatedly do. Excellence, then, is not an act but a habit".
~ Aristotle ~

In 1989 George started The Mpala Wildlife Foundation, dedicated to preserving the wildlife and the resources of the Laikipia region of Kenya. Encompassing 48,000 acres of land, the foundation provided important protection of the wildlife, the people and a way of life. In 1991 the Kenyan Wildlife Service, The National Museums of Kenya, Princeton University, and the Smithsonian Institute entered into a partnership with George to create a research center on a portion of the ranch. Mpala Research Centre, Mpala Conservancy and the Mpala mobile clinic were born.

George Small died in 2002 from brain cancer but his legacy lives on in the people providing healing services to the Laikipia and Samburu regions of Kenya. By 2003, the medical clinic had already touched over 100,000 souls who otherwise would have no access to professional medical care. By 2007, The Community Health Africa Trust (CHAT) absorbed the Mpala outreach services and continues to provided inoculations, disease prevention, and other medical needs to the poverty stricken areas of northern Kenya. Even today, these mobile services reach people by any means necessary- by foot, camel convoy, truck or bicycle.

In 1983, Ethiopia was experiencing the beginnings of a historic drought. What I saw was just the beginning of a catastrophe that would grow into one of the biggest disasters Africa has ever known. By 1984, it had become a humanitarian crisis on a biblical scale, estimating to have claimed 500,000-1,000,000 lives from starvation. In response, the world stepped in with relief in the form of Live Aid, raising money and awareness through concerts in the United States, Great Britain and beyond. On July 13, 1985 the concerts would raise over $283,000,000. to aid the Ethiopian disaster.

Simon Evans continued his safari work and eventually built a new home and subsequent lodge overlooking the Ewaso Nyiro River which flows out of the highlands and through to the dry plains of

Samburu. Named *Sabuk* (tsavok), meaning 'river' in
Maasai, it is operating today as an eco-lodge,
highlighted by camel safaris through the bush. It is too
bad that I never met his father, Jasper Evans, because
apparently he was one of the most interesting and
infamous characters in Kenya. Jasper died in February
2010. In 2013, I finally got in touch with Simon, who is
just a few years older than me. I trust he has many years
ahead of him to do good work.

Ivory poaching has been illegal since 1973.
Despite that, the corruption around 'blood ivory' in
Kenya runs deep, including government officials. In the
1970s, Ngina Kenyatta, wife of then President Jomo
Kenyatta and other high-level government officials
were allegedly involved in an ivory-smuggling ring that
transported tusks out of the country in the state's
private airplane. There is documented proof that at
least one member of Kenya's royal family had shipped
over six tons of ivory to China. By the late 1970s, the
elephant population was estimated around 275,000,
dropping to 20,000 in 1989.

Daniel Arap Moi, Kenya's president from 1978
until 2002, was no more successful in stemming the tide
of slaughter and, in fact, fanned the flame of doubt.
After the August 1, 1982 uprising against him in Naiobi,
Moi brought back the 'detain without cause' law. He
detained seven innocent people in early 1983, including
four lecturers from the University of Nairobi and their

lawyer. When I was there in the summer of 1983, the election for the president was pushed forward by fourteen months to September that year in direct response to the coup of 1982.

In 1989, in an attempt to demonstrate international solidarity against ivory poaching, he ordered twelve tons of ivory to be set on fire. Regardless, throughout Moi's reign reports of human rights abuses, bribes, and cover-ups finally caught up with him and he was barred from running again in 2002.

In addition to ongoing questions of insider involvement around illegal ivory, Kenya tried to down play a series of murders in the late 1980's. Five tourists in 1988 were killed by poachers turned bandits, including a Connecticut woman. Then in August 1989, George Adamson of *Born Free* fame, was murdered along with his two assistants at his campsite by poachers. Sadly, Mrs. Joy Adamson had also been murdered in 1980. In her case, by one of her own camp staff.

And then there was Julie Ward- the most well-publicized murder victim of all. While on tour in the Maasai Mara Reserve in 1988, she wandered away from camp and was never seen again. Her body was found burned and dismembered in the bush. Questions about who actually killed Julie persisted for the better part of twenty years. Thanks to her determined father from

Scotland Yard, the case finally pointed back to Jonathan Moi, the president's son, who was accused of raping and murdering Julie despite government attempts to cover it up.

I would discover that the little town of Voi outside Tsavo, where we had the encounter with baboons, was near the Voi airport where the famous Denys Fitch Hatton took off for the last time. Tsavo was one of Denys Fitch Hatton's favorite places and he would die there alongside his servant, Hamisi, when his Gypsy Moth plane crashed in Tsavo on May 14, 1931. There is a camp erected in Denys's name in Tsavo simply called *Fitch- Hatton's* which still operates today. Karen Blixen would help memorialize him in her book; *Out of Africa* which became a movie in 1985. The Voi gas station closed in the early 1990's but in short order nature took it back. The baboons are still there- they have made it their own.

When I got back, art became my career as well as a passion. Sam Shriver, father to Pam Shriver the tennis pro, was one of my first clients. He commissioned me to do a reticulated giraffe for his wife after a trip to Mpala. I just recently got in touch with Pam Shriver to confirm this. Sam Shriver died in 2006 of lung cancer.

I incorporated as The Perrine Company in 1988. After doing African wildlife for many years, I was able to conquer almost every medium and every type of painting- murals, holiday cards, architectural rendering, painted furniture, and more. For a short while, The Perrine Company became a shop where I provided framing and paintings, plus custom painted furniture in the mid- nineties.

In the early nineties Dr. Lurie and I crossed paths one day at a dinner dance event in Baltimore. I recognized him but he did not recognize me. After I explained who I was, he was amazed at how I looked and how well I had recovered from the staph infection. Happily, there are no residual effects from the surgery, thanks to him. He still practices oral surgery and facial reconstruction today.

I was married in 1991 and had two remarkable children, Emilia and Lee, in the late 1990's. Unfortunately my dad, Arthur Lee Shreve III., died in 1995 of lung cancer and was never able to meet my children.

My mother, Anne Obrecht Shreve, is still living. My sister, Leslie Shreve, is also a small business owner and entrepreneur and is bringing her gifts to the world. Eventually divorced in 2008, the ultimate reinvention of myself began. Through this period of growth and expansion my transformation led me to become a certified wellness coach, personal trainer and thought leader in healthy behavior. I started a new business; Lifeguard Wellness, and created tools that could show others another way to become who they were meant to be.

In 2009, I was able to reach Dr. Howard Erickson, who had retired from the zoology department at Towson University. Howard and I compared notes and memories. He was able to clarify the details of my release and confirm other information for this book. Still vital at almost eighty, he has scaled Mt. Kenya many times and continues to travel to East Africa. In fact, when I spoke with him last, he was off to Tanzania in June of 2012.

July 2011 brought another inferno of burning ivory ordered by, now president, Mwai Kibaki. Five tons of contraband ivory worth 16 million USD was reclaimed from Singapore and other countries and set on fire.

Kenya experienced another rise in black market exportation of ivory and slaughtering of elephants in 2012 that reached a fever pitch. Ivory was selling at an all-time high in price of $105.per pound. Two fifty pound tusks are worth over $10,000. - an incredible fortune to most Kenyans whose average earnings are equal to under $1,000.USD per year.

A report came out of Africa on January 12, 2013 that Kenya had seen its worst attack on elephants to date; a family of twelve hunted down for their tusks. Their tusks hacked out of their faces, ironically in Tsavo National Park. Now, more than ever, the destiny of elephants and the strength of the fibers in an unraveling veil of protection is in question.

Still without last names, I have not been able to find any of my fellow travelers. The one journal that I wrote in on my return is still missing. I do not know where my paintings of Mpala ended up, but I trust they are in good hands. *Kwa heri.*

ACKNOWLEDGEMENTS

"Individuals shape society but collaboration moves the world."
~ Pete Kohlasch ~

No man is an island, especially when it comes to writing a book. It is always a collaboration which has ripples that emanate out in many different directions — a confluence of ideas, thoughts, inspiration, support and research that runs the gamut. May I just say to everyone– thank you from the bottom of my heart!

First, if it had not been for Dr. Howard Erickson there would not be a memoir of my journey. His vast experience in Africa and zoology made it possible for us to go to Kenya in 1983 in the first place, and now, with his input and confirmation of my memories, it has come to life! I will be forever indebted to him for sharing his knowledge and passion for Africa.

Many thanks to Darsi Ruysenaar, who I found with the help of The Muthiaga Club in Nairobi. We connected in the summer of 2012. Darsi not only organized the safari itinerary for the first trip but helped me almost thirty years later to piece together some of the lost details. He has added rich historic layers from his own family history, valuable insight, plus political perspective which otherwise would have been lost. And to his brother, Hans, who in 2012 from South Africa, helped me via Skype with more historical perspective on the settlement of Kenya before W.W. II and family details.

I am very thankful for my editor, Susan Scher, who made the text flow and gave me indispensable advice on how to be a better writer. Thanks go out to Sara Sgarlatt for her input and guidance, and to Patricia Maranga Redsicker from Kenya, now living in the USA, for her in-depth knowledge of the country and perspective.

Jonathan Luckin, my new young friend and intern, was able to finish this manuscript right- with the proper formatting and give it polish. Without him, it wouldn't have been ready on time.

I am grateful for my friend and fellow writer, Pete Kohlasch, for his thoughtful and profound quotes which were a perfect match to this story. And then there is the encouragement from my friend, John Brandon Sills– one of the best plein air painters in the country, who helped facilitate the evolution of my art into the style which appears in this story.

Thanks to my new friend, Margrit Harris, who agreed to write the Foreword, and is as passionate about Africa as I am. And thanks to all who added their own testimonials and praise, time and attention.

I will never forget all my friends and family who created a bridge through troubled waters, kept the faith and helped me get to the other side. I do not know where I would be without you.

And finally, I appreciate the endless story telling advice and great input from my dear friend and confidante, Kim Reese, who never got tired of hearing the story. She helped me hone it to a finer and finer point with her sharp intellect and writing prowess. Her support and strong belief in me was much needed at times to get this book to press. Thank you, my sweet friend.

God Bless you all,

Heather

Finding The Fire Within

ABOUT THE AUTHOR

Heather Perrine Shreve

Underneath the Words ~ Behind the Brush

In the words of John Muir, *"Everybody needs beauty as well as bread, places to play in and pray in, where nature may heal and give strength to body and soul."* Intuitively, this has been Heather's perspective and belief since she was very young and continues to perpetuate these ideals through her pursuits; her writing and art.

The decision to write this important part of her life story came after the economic downturn of October, 2008 when her twenty year professional art business faltered. At age 45, Heather decided to change careers and so a new company, Lifeguard Wellness, was born.

At the same time, in May 2009, she began putting her memories of Africa on paper- for her children and before too much time had passed. In the country's current sea of uncertainty, Heather thought the timing was right and began writing <u>Caught On The Equator, Finding The Fire Within</u> for anyone who would enjoy an adventure about a teenager in an exotic country with her own uncertainty.

So, with only the formal training in literature she received in high school, Heather took on the challenge of writing a memoir in the form of a creative narrative that reads more like a novel. Working at a steady pace and using the internet for research and to find key people, four years later the art and the manuscript were complete.

As a lifetime artist, Heather has also logged more than 30,000 hours behind the brush. In her career as a professional artist her clients ranged from large companies like McCormick Spice, CSX, and Sheraton Hotels to the city of Baltimore, the state of Maryland and former Governor Bob Ehrlich. Heather has been commissioned to do hundreds of paintings in her lifetime so far. Individual clients have asked her to paint everything from eighty foot murals to illustrating custom children's stories. Fluid in many mediums, Heather's ability for detail can be seen in her architectural renderings as well as in a birds' feather. For this book, the acrylic paintings on board were done with an underlayment of swirled gesso to give the images a rough appearance, like the textures of Africa. In addition- only the three primary colors were used plus black and white.

Going forward, Heather's wish is to help wildlife conservation in Africa, especially the plight of the elephants with the sales from this book. The messages in *Caught On The Equator* are also pivotal to Heather's work in public health and well-being, in all its forms. Her focus is on thought patterns and how it affects not just physical health but emotional, mental and spiritual resilience. As a certified Wellcoach™ (ACSM) and human behavior specialist, she pursues these principles with this book and her two health workbooks: *Drawn Into Wellness* and *Doodle Yourself 2 Health,* also on Amazon.

Finding The Fire Within

MARGRIT HARRIS

The Nikela Foundation

Margrit Harris, who was born in South Africa, came to the United States to marry her future husband. Once there, Margrit raised three children, worked as a psychotherapist and later ran her own management consulting firm focused on creating effective teams for financial advisors. In early 2010, Margrit and her husband, Russ, founded Nikela after a trip to visit Margrit's parents in South Africa. *Nikela*, which means "give to" in Zulu, was born out of the desire to create a vehicle for wildlife lovers around the world to get involved and make a difference by making a small donation and/or volunteering a few hours.

Nikela helps those who protect Africa's wildlife from poachers and other threats, as well as campaigning to stop the buying of illegally traded wildlife and their body parts.

Nikela is a public charity with 501 (c)(3) status, that operates virtually so that anyone anywhere who cares to give can. 100% of online donations go to the projects. We can do this because we operate via the time and expertise donated by volunteers from around the globe.

Today, due to the dire need to stop the illegal poaching and trading of wildlife, Nikela's focus has narrowed to 1) support those who stop the wildlife poachers and 2) educate young and old to end the buying of exotic wildlife and products made from wildlife body parts, like fur, skin, bones, horns, tusks, etc.

Our vision is to see a world where wildlife is not threatened and children have hope, made possible by a community of compassionate people giving to those who protect our planet's wildlife and prepare the rising generation to do the same. Our mission is to protect now and educate for the future, via rescue and rehabilitation, anti-poaching, advocacy, and providing sanctuary and educate via live educational programs, online resources, and international awareness campaigns. Nikela finds and qualifies experts and certifies wildlife conservation and education projects. Donors choose and give to the ones that particularly appeal to them. Experts protect the wildlife and educate others, especially children, to do the same.

If we all join together, we can make a huge difference. If you care for wildlife, want to protect it and help kids find their place in doing the same, you may want to join us. NIKELA provides a rewarding way to do it.

INDEX OF PAINTINGS
By Heather P. Shreve

BIBLIOGRAPHY

"AllAfrica." *AllAfrica.com: Kenya: Jonathan Moi Denies Killing Julie Ward*. N.p., n.d. Web. 13 Jan. 2013.

"Elephant Hunting in Kenya." *Wikipedia*. Wikimedia Foundation, 12 Sept. 2012. Web. 13 Jan. 2013.

"Family of 11 Elephants Slaughtered by Poachers in Kenya." *CCTV News*. N.p., n.d. Web. 13 Jan. 2013.

"OnTheFlyExpeditions.com." *OnTheFlyExpeditions.com*. N.p., n.d. Web. 13 Jan. 2013.

Times, Jane Perlez, Special To The New York. "George Adamson, Lions' Protector, Is Shot Dead by Bandits in Kenya." *The New York Times*. The New York Times, 22 Aug. 1989. Web. 12 Jan. 2013.

"Kenya Burns Ivory in Fight against Poachers." *BBC News*. BBC, 20 July 2011. Web. 22 Jan. 2013.

"Jambonewspot." *Jambonewspot RSS*. N.p., n.d. Web. 12 Feb. 2013.

RESOURCES

The Nikela Foundation, Founders ~ Margrit and Russ
Harris
The Big Life Foundation, Founder ~ Nick Brandt
Strategic Protection of Threatened Species (SPOTS),
Founder ~ Peter Milton
Campaign Against Canned Hunting (CACH), Founder
~ Chris Mercer
Silent Heroes Foundation, Founder ~ Hayley Adams
African Bird of Prey Sanctuary (ABOPS),
Founder ~ Shannon Hoffman
Daktari Bush School, Founder ~ Michele Merrifield
Bambelela, Primate Rescue and Rehab, Founder ~ Silke
Van Eynern
World Wildlife Fund
Wildaid
The Sierra Club, Founder ~ John Muir
The Nature Conservancy
Oceanna
Conservation International
The Royal Society for the Protection of Birds
The Wildlife Conservation Society

Finding The Fire Within

Made in the USA
Charleston, SC
05 June 2013